Going on to Salvation

Going on to Salvation

REVISED EDITION

A Study of Wesleyan Beliefs

Maxie Dunnam

A guide for the Christian pilgrimage of
"faith working through love," as envisioned by
John Wesley and practiced by the people called Methodist

Abingdon Press
Nashville

GOING ON TO SALVATION
A STUDY OF WESLEYAN BELIEFS

This book is printed on acid-free paper.

Library of Congress Cataloging-in-Publication Data

Dunnam, Maxie D.
Going on to salvation : a study of Wesleyan beliefs / Maxie Dunnam.
p. cm.
ISBN 978-0-687-65313-3 (binding: pbk., adhesive, perfect : alk. paper)
1. Salvation—Christianity. 2. Wesley, John 1703–1791. 3. Methodist Church—Doctrines.
I. Title.

BT751.3.D86 2008
230′.76—dc22

2008033916

08 09 10 11 12 13 14 15 16 17—10 9 8 7 6 5 4 3 2 1

MANUFACTURED IN THE UNITED STATES OF AMERICA

TO

The Reverend David H. McKeithen, who brought me into the Methodist fold and guided my first stumbling steps in the ministry;

TO

The congregation of Christ United Methodist Church, Memphis, Tennessee, who called forth the best that is in me as preacher, allowed me the joy of being their pastor, and supported me with their prayers and mutual ministry—to whom the basic content of this book was preached to launch our celebration of the Bicentennial Year of Methodism in America;

AND TO

Methodist congregations I have served in McLain, Beaumont, Leaf, Avant, Gautier, and Gulfport, Mississippi; Atlanta, Georgia; San Clemente and Anaheim, California. "I thank my God upon every remembrance of you."

CONTENTS

Introduction

In my introduction to the first edition of this book, I shared a bit of my Christian journey. I'm a United Methodist by choice.

I was converted in a little Southern Baptist church in rural Mississippi and baptized at the hands of Brother Wiley Grissom in a rather cold creek in early September. My mother and father were active in that church, and my father served as a deacon.

I knew only one Catholic before I went to college. He was a normal sort of fellow, but we thought it strange that he and his family would drive thirty miles each Sunday to get to a Catholic church for mass. Interestingly, Roman Catholic writers have been primary sources of spiritual nurture for me; and one of the most meaningful relationships I have had was with the Ecumenical Institute of Spirituality—twenty-five persons, among whom are eight Roman Catholics, along with Quakers, Orthodox Christians, Episcopalians, Lutherans, Presbyterians, and others.

I became a Methodist by choice about three years after my conversion. Doctrine had a lot to do with it—style also. But I wouldn't diminish the influence of a Methodist preacher, David McKeithen, a warm, loving human being who cared deeply for people and preached the gospel thoughtfully and with deep conviction. I began to feel the call to preach, and I felt that should I ever answer that call, I ought to be in the "right" church for me. I began to read and talk to people, and eventually made the choice, surprising David and his congregation when I walked down the aisle on a Sunday morning to offer myself as a member. Then, a year later, I offered myself to that same congregation as a "candidate for ministry."

So I'm a United Methodist by choice. My purpose in writing the book originally was to make clear the way of salvation as understood and experienced in the Wesleyan movement. This was not to be a reasoned apologetic for Wesleyan/Arminian theology. It was an effort on my part to present what I believe is the "heartbeat," the distinct content, and, to some degree, the style of who we are as Methodists.

That was over two decades ago. During the years since, there has been a resurgence of Calvinism, the branch of evangelical Protestantism that is markedly different in doctrine from the Methodist/Wesleyan way. Disputes between Calvinism and its critics have raged throughout church history, certainly since the time of Augustine. Jerry Walls and Joe Dongell, in their book *Why I Am Not a Calvinist,* noted that in the past several decades Calvinism seemed largely to have lost the battle, at least in America. Various forms of Arminian, Wesleyan, and Pentecostal theology began to dominate evangelicalism in the twentieth century. Even though there were strong, articulate advocates, and outstanding educational institutions and publishing enterprises clearly identified with Calvinism, "it seemed to be fighting a losing battle in the modern and post-modern church" (p. 13).

Now Calvinism is making a remarkable comeback. This is seen in the leadership of the Southern Baptist Convention, the largest Protestant denomination in the United States, and it is chronicled by Keith Hinson in a *Christianity Today* article entitled "Calvinism Resurging among SBC's Young Elites" (October 6, 1997), and by Ernest C. Reisinger and D. Matthew Allen, in *A Quiet Revolution: A Chronicle of Beginnings of Reformation in the Southern Baptist Convention* (Cape Coral, FL: Founders, 2000).

The resurgence is seen among young persons, especially college students. There are a number of universities and colleges where the most dynamic campus ministry is Reformed University Fellowship. Some of the most popular bands among college students are openly Reformed in theological perspective. John Piper, one of the most outstanding proponents of classic Calvinism, is the most popular speaker at the gatherings of the college youth movement called Passion. The resurgence is also seen in a constant stream of books and magazines championing the Calvinist cause.

As I travel the country, speaking, teaching, leading conferences and retreats, I am regularly involved in conversation with persons who are asking questions about our Methodist/Wesleyan doctrine, specifically in relation to the Calvinist understanding of the sovereignty of God, free will, the nature of grace, predestination and salvation, and eternal security. As the publisher and I considered a new edition of this book, I was convinced that I needed to speak specifically about our Methodist/Wesleyan distinctiveness in relation to Calvinism.

So there are two changes in this edition. One, I have sought to eliminate dated material and provide some more contemporary illustrations. Two, I have added a chapter that will address the Methodist/Calvinist issue. In this added chapter, I will deal only with the obvious, unavoidable distinctions that greatly affect how we practice our Christian discipleship, how we provide pastoral care for one another (especially the pastor), and how we understand mission and evangelism. My desire is that this brief presentation will give laypersons and clergy more confidence in their witness and everyday conversation, that there will be enough here to prevent the reader from being intimidated by the aggressiveness of the Calvinist apologist, and that we will find encouragement to immerse ourselves more fully in our Methodist/Wesleyan way, as well as to understand more clearly the Calvinist position.[1]

The central theme of each chapter will be rooted in a particular scripture passage. This is done deliberately to underscore Wesley's claim that he was a person of "one Book," and to call us Methodists back to the primary source of our life as individuals and in the church. A recovery of an emphasis upon scripture is one of the crucial needs in Methodism.

I have also deliberately quoted Wesley frequently. We need to read Wesley more if we are going to be faithful to our heritage; but more, we need to read him in order to capture the same spirit that controlled his life and brought revival to England and America. Yet I have also sought to put the message into our contemporary setting and our experiential need.

It is my prayer that this effort will make a contribution to the renewal of our church as we discover, or rediscover, the unique place we have in God's family. We need to recover that uniqueness, not to set us apart from others, but that we might be the people God wants us to be. God would be pleased, I think, if we would take up again, with commitment, zeal, and dependence upon the Holy Spirit, that mission which was declared when the Methodist movement first put its roots down in this new land: to reform a continent and spread scriptural holiness across the land.

For each chapter I have devised a set of questions for personal reflection and a separate set of questions to guide group sharing. The design is that you will not read this book at one sitting, or even over a period of a few days. I hope that you will take it slowly as you read each chapter, taking time to ponder and study the questions for personal reflection. Use the space provided at the end of each chapter to write your reflections when I ask you to do that. If you wish to write more extended answers, keep a separate notebook as your personal journal.

The Wesleyan expression of our Christian faith is experiential. Reading the book, and responding to the questions for personal reflection, will assist you in getting in touch with your own spiritual pilgrimage experientially.

There is also a set of questions for each chapter to guide group sharing. If you use the book as a group study resource, these questions will be helpful in your regular discussion gatherings.

My suggestion is that the leader of the group (and leadership may change for each session) read the questions ahead of time and select the ones that should have priority in your particular group. Again, however, questions for each group meeting call for the sharing of personal experience, not just ideas and content. You will miss the potential richness of this adventure unless you give that priority. John Wesley said the meaning of Christian fellowship is one loving heart setting another on fire. We do that primarily by sharing our personal journeys.

Naturally, I am pleased that this book is being released now in a revised edition. Since it was originally published in 1984, it has been printed in three editions and translated into at least six languages. My prayer is that the reader will grasp more fully the richness of the Wesleyan Way and become more confident in the gospel.

Maxie Dunnam
Eastertide, 2008

---

[1]To pursue the dialogue more deliberately I recommend two books: *Why I Am Not a Calvinist*, by Jerry L. Walls and Joseph R. Dongell; and *Arminian Theology: Myths and Realities*, by Roger E. Olson.

CHAPTER 1

THE KEYSTONE: SALVATION BY FAITH

You were dead through the trespasses and sins in which you once lived. . . . But God, who is rich in mercy, out of the great love with which he loved us even when we were dead through our trespasses, made us alive together with Christ—by grace you have been saved—and raised us up with him and seated us with him in the heavenly places in Christ Jesus, so that in the ages to come he might show the immeasurable riches of his grace in kindness toward us in Christ Jesus. For by grace you have been saved through faith, and this is not your own doing; it is the gift of God—not the result of works, so that no one may boast. For we are what he has made us, created in Christ Jesus for good works, which God prepared beforehand to be our way of life.

(Ephesians 2:1, 2, 4-10)

If you were asked, "What is the goal of your life?" how would you respond? To be happy? To have a healthy, happy family? To be a success in business? To be wealthy? To serve other people and make others happy? To find the right marriage mate? To be fulfilled in your profession? Listen to the founder of Methodism, John Wesley:

> To candid, reasonable men, I'm not afraid to lay open what have been the inmost thoughts of my heart. I have thought, I'm a creature of a day, passing through life as an arrow through the air. I am a spirit come from God, and returning to God: Just hovering over the great gulf; til a few

> moments hence, I am no more seen; I drop into an unchangeable eternity. I want to know one thing—the way to heaven; how to land safe on that happy shore. God himself has condescended to teach the way; for this very end He came from heaven. He hath written it down in a book. O give me that book! At any price, give me the Book of God! (*John Wesley's Fifty-Three Sermons,* edited by Edward H. Sugden [Nashville: Abingdon Press, 1983]. This quotation is taken from the Preface to the Sermons.)

This word expressed the fire burning in Wesley's soul: "I want to know one thing—the way to heaven—how to land safe on that happy shore." This desire of Wesley was like that passionate expression of Paul to the Philippians:

> Not that I have already obtained this or have already reached the goal; but I press on to make it my own, because Christ Jesus has made me his own. Beloved, I do not consider that I have made it my own; but this one thing I do: forgetting what lies behind and straining forward to what lies ahead, I press on toward the goal for the prize of the heavenly call of God in Christ Jesus. (Philippians 3:12-14)

The goal of Wesley's life was his own salvation. History verifies that once he was certain of that—his own salvation—the passion became other-directed, and he started one of the great revivals of history as he sought to share the salvation message with others. Over and over in this *Journal,* he records his preaching activity in his simple sentence: "I offered them Christ."

John Wesley published four volumes of sermons—in 1746, 1748, 1750, and 1760. In 1763, he prepared a model deed for his preaching houses that set forth his intentions after his death. In that deed, it was provided that persons appointed by the conference should "have and enjoy the premises" only on condition "that the said persons preach no other doctrine than is contained in Mr. Wesley's Notes upon the New Testament and four volumes of sermons" (*John Wesley's Fifty-Three Sermons,* Ibid.; p. 1).

"Salvation by faith" was the first of Wesley's *standard sermons.* So this is where we begin, the keystone of his understanding of Christian doctrine—"salvation by faith."

Paul developed this theme systematically in his Letter to the Romans. His Galatians letter was an expression of the same truth primarily from his heart, not his head. Our scripture from Ephesians is a spontaneous outpouring of this conviction about salvation by faith in the midst of a commentary on the nature and mission of the church.

Since Paul, volumes have been written on this theme of salvation by faith; and I boldly propose to capture the essence of it (at least enough for us to go on) in this chapter by asking, in the style of Mr. Wesley's sermon on this theme, three questions:

One, who needs it?
Two, what is it we need?
Three, how do we get it?

WHO NEEDS SALVATION?

First, who needs it? The answer is clear, simple, and encompassing: we all need it.

Paul stated our predicament: "You were dead through the trespasses and sins in which you once lived, following the course of this world, following the ruler of the power of the air, the spirit that is now at work among those who are disobedient" (Ephesians 2:1-2).

In Romans 3, Paul deals specifically with the universality of sin, quoting passages from five psalms and one verse from Isaiah. Consider his terrible word:

"There is no one who is righteous, not even one;
there is no one who has understanding,
there is no one who seeks God.
All have turned aside, together they have become worthless;
there is no one who shows kindness,
there is not even one."
"Their throats are opened graves;
they use their tongues to deceive."
"The venom of vipers is under their lips."
"Their mouths are full of cursing and bitterness."
"Their feet are swift to shed blood;
ruin and misery are in their paths,
and the way of peace they have not known."
"There is no fear of God before their eyes."
(Romans 3:10-18)

Paul begins this catalog of our common predicament by contending that we are all under sin. Think about that for a moment. Wesley was as adamant as Paul. Sin is universal. Likewise, as we will discuss later, the offer of salvation is universal. As all have sinned and come short of the glory of God (Romans 3:23), all are offered the saving grace of Jesus Christ. There is a sense in which Wesley's understanding of salvation is summed up in four "alls": *all need to be saved; all may be saved; all may know they are saved; all may be saved to the uttermost.*

In Romans 3:9, Paul contends that everyone, "both Jews and Greeks, are under the power of sin." The Greek phrase that Paul uses for this state of being under sin when we are without Christ is *hypo harmartian*, and it means "in the power of" or "under the authority of" sin. You get the scope of it by seeing the way Paul uses that phrase in other places: he described the relationship between a schoolboy and his teacher in Galatians 3:25 (KJV) as being "under a schoolmaster." In 1 Timothy 6:1, he said slaves were "under the yoke." In both these instances, to be "under" means to be dominated by or under the authority of.

That's the predicament of all of us. Paul summed it up: "For there is no distinction, since all have sinned and fall short of the glory of God" (Romans 3:22-23).

Do you have problems believing that? Is the description Paul uses too terrible? In another chapter, we will deal with the whole issue of "original sin." For now, let's not debate the universality of sin, but seek to see where we are in the picture. Without dealing with such glaring sins as adultery, killing, and stealing, answer these questions:

- Do you sometimes think more highly of yourself than you ought to think?
- Is there any person of whom you are jealous?
- Do you occasionally look at a person of the opposite sex and feel lust in your heart?
- Do you sometimes hate people of other races or nations?
- Do you get anxious about the future because you feel you don't have enough financial security?
- Do you judge others by what they have? By their station in life? Whether they are cultured or not? Their level of educational achievement?

When the publisher and I decided to publish this new edition of the book, I wanted a couple of my friends who are Wesley scholars to read the original edition to offer any suggestions they thought helpful. The book was out of print, so I had to order used copies online for them to have a text to read. In one of the used copies, the original owner had made notes. After the first of the above questions, he had written "sometimes." After the second question, he named the person he was jealous of; and he put a "yes" after the other questions.

The questions seem innocent enough, but, like the reader, most of us would answer yes to a number of them. Do you know what that means? It means that we are among those Paul was describing: "All have sinned and fall short of the glory of God."

So who needs it? Who needs salvation? We all do!

WHAT SALVATION DO WE NEED?

Now, the second question: What is it we need? We need salvation. What is the nature of this salvation?

Let's take our cue directly from scripture. Paul describes the result of sin in our life: "You were dead through . . . trespasses and sins." You were not in control of your life—you followed "the course of this world" like a puppet controlled by Satan. This means that you lived in "the passion of your flesh, following the desires of body and mind."

But then something happened. God "made us alive together with Christ." It's a dramatic distinction. Sin equals death—you were dead; salvation equals life—God made us live. This is an echo of Paul's whole life. He knew himself to be a great sinner, but he knew Christ to be a great Savior. He never understated or underplayed sin in our lives; nor did he understate or underplay the redeeming power of Jesus Christ. So it was with John Wesley.

The salvation we need and the salvation Christ affords is the salvation from sin. Be clear about this. It is a *present* salvation. Paul did not say to the Ephesians, "You *will* be saved." He said, "You *have been* saved." The work is accomplished now. Let us see how this happens at the point of three great needs:

First, it is a salvation from *the guilt of all past sins*. Paul put it graphically in Colossians 2:1-14. We have been forgiven all our sins; "the record that stood against us with its legal demands" has been set aside, cancelled, *nailed to the cross*. What a descriptive metaphor . . . nailed to the cross.

Sometimes the setting in which we read scripture adds special meaning to it. I was using William Barclay's Daily Study Bible of Galatians for my daily devotional reading when I first visited China in 1967. I came to the third chapter the day I entered the country. "O senseless Galatians, who has put the evil eye on you—you before whose very eyes Jesus was placarded upon his cross?" (v. l, *Barclay*). I like the New Living Translation rendering of this verse: "Oh, foolish Galatians! What magician has cast an evil spell on you? For you used to see the meaning of Jesus Christ's death as clearly as though I had shown you a signboard with a picture of Christ dying on the cross."

It was clear to me when I arrived that China was a land of posters. This was in a more primitive communication day, and posters and placards were everywhere. Crowds would gather around the walls where newsprint and posters were displayed. A primary means of communication, posters were used to share the message of liberation and revolution in that vast land.

The Greek word that Barclay translates "placarded" in Galatians 3:1 is *prographein*. It is one of the words Paul used for preaching, and it meant "post a notice," as on a bulletin board in a public square. This is why it came through to me with such power in China. Barclay reminded us that in New Testament times the word was used to describe what a father did when he proclaimed publicly that he would no longer be responsible for his son's debts.

In the same fashion, but conveying the opposite message, Jesus Christ, placarded upon his cross, has been portrayed among the Galatians. The message posted on the bulletin boards of our hearts is not that the Father will no longer be responsible for our debts, but that through the crucified Christ he has paid our debts.

Paul and other New Testament writers used a lot of other images to describe the way of our salvation: release from bondage, satisfaction for our sins, reconciliation, the old Adam dying and the new Adam coming to life. Whatever the image, the truth is clear. The central message of the New Testament is that in the cross, Christ has done something for us that we cannot do for ourselves. He has "[erased] the record that stood against us," thus freeing us.

Can anything be more dramatic or powerful . . . to know that when Jesus was nailed to the cross, our sins, my sins, your sins, and the guilt therefrom was nailed to the cross? I see this demonstrated over and over again. Here is a picture of it.

A fifty-year-old woman—let's call her Mary—was devastated with guilt over estrangement from and hatred of her father. Mary's mother had died of cancer. During the last months of her mother's life, Mary's father had courted, and married almost immediately after the death of his wife, another woman. Mary's hatred for her father and his new wife was venomous. She refused to see or have anything to do with them. She finally came to see that hatred was destroying her. Then she became plagued with guilt over fifteen years of estrangement from her father. Her guilt paralyzed her. She wanted reconciliation, but she could not take the initiative in the relationship. The father had given up long ago.

At the close of a worship service where the theme of forgiveness—salvation from all past sin and guilt—had been proclaimed, Mary and I shared and prayed together for about an hour. Mary believed, accepted the forgiveness of grace, and claimed salvation for herself. That very night she wrote to her father, and began the process of reconciliation and the reclaiming and rebuilding of a daughter-father love and relationship.

Second, we are saved not only from the guilt of all past sins; *we are also saved from fear*. Fear is the twin of guilt and burns almost as ravaging as guilt itself in many of our lives—fear of God's judgment, of eternal punishment, of God's wrath.

But the salvation Christ affords takes away our fear. We now know not the wrath of God, but God's extravagant love. We "have not received the spirit of bondage again to fear; . . . but . . . the Spirit of adoption, whereby we cry, Abba, Father. The Spirit itself beareth witness with our spirit, that we are the children of God" (Romans 8:15-16 KJV).

John Wesley would remind us that we are also saved from the fear, though not from the possibility, of falling away from the grace of God and coming short of God's great and precious promises. That is a unique understanding of Methodism. We will return to it later. We are saved from the fear, though not the possibility, of falling away from the grace of God. We are "sealed with the promised Holy Spirit, which is the guarantee of our inheritance" (Ephesians 1:13 RSV). So we have peace with God through our Lord Jesus Christ. We rejoice in the hope of the glory of God, and the love of God is shed abroad in our hearts, through the Holy Spirit, which is given to us. And hereby we are persuaded, though perhaps not at all times, nor with the same fullness of persuasion, that neither death nor life, nor things present nor things to come, nor height, nor depth, nor any creature shall be able to separate us from the love of God, which is in Christ Jesus our Lord.

We are saved from fear.

Third, the last word about the nature of our salvation is that we are *saved from the power of sin.* We *will* discuss this in the chapter on sanctification, but it must be noted now. Paul was very clear about the fact that unredeemed persons live under the power of sin. He was also triumphantly clear about the fact that Christ frees us from the power of sin. "He has rescued us from the power of darkness and transferred us into the kingdom of his beloved Son" (Colossians 1:13).

In his sermon on "Salvation by Faith," Wesley made the case emphatically:

> Those who by faith are born of God do not continue in sin. (1) They are no longer in bondage to besetting sins that stem from the reign of sin in the heart. Sin no longer rules the lives of Christian believers. (2) Believers are no longer captives to willful sin. So long as they continue in faith, sin is as abhorrent to them as a deadly poison. (3) Christians lose their lust for sin because they now desire the holy and perfect will of God. By God's grace, tendencies toward unholy desires can be resisted as soon as they arise. (4) Those human infirmities that are neither deliberate nor intentional may cause us to fall short. But if they are neither deliberate nor intentional, they are not properly considered as sins. Therefore, 'No one who is born of God will continue to sin.' Although Christian believers cannot claim that they have never sinned, they no longer need to be subject to sin's power. (*John Wesley on Christian Beliefs: The Standard Sermons in Modern English*, vol. 1, Kenneth Cain Kinghorn, Abingdon Press, 2002; p. 41)

This was John Wesley's deep conviction. His brother, Charles, sang joyfully about this fact:

> Long my imprisoned spirit lay,
> Fast bound in sin and nature's night;
> Thine eye diffused a quickening ray;
> I woke, the dungeon flamed with light;
> My chains fell off, my heart was free,
> I rose, went forth, and followed thee.
> *(The United Methodist Hymnal, #363)*

So what is it we need? Salvation that is a present reality—salvation from sin, from the guilt and fear that result from sin, and from sin's power over us.

HOW DO WE RECEIVE SALVATION?

Now, the final question: *How do we get salvation?* The answer is this: we don't get it; *it is given.*

Isn't it strange that we have as many problems with this fact as any other? One of the crucial debates of Christian doctrine has swirled around this issue. How are we to be saved? Two common theories have been set forth as to how we are reconciled to God: one is by *works*, the other by *faith*. We underscore again Paul's words from Ephesians 2:8-9: "For by grace you have been saved through faith, and this is not your own doing; it is the gift of God—not the result of works, so that no one may boast." How do we get it? We don't; it is given. Salvation is by faith and faith alone."

In Romans 3:23-25, Paul states the truth about salvation as a gift in this fashion: "Since all have sinned and fall short of the glory of God, they are justified by his grace as a gift, through the redemption which is in Christ Jesus, whom God put forward as an expiation by his blood, to be received by faith" (RSV). The Greek word for expiation "refers to the sacrifices offered to pagan deities, as a means of appeasing their displeasure and averting their anger." Some theologians transferred this concept to the New Testament and saw Christ's sacrifice as a means of placating an angry God. Others have objected to this interpretation on the grounds that it demeans God's nature, that it reduces God to the level of a petty pagan deity.

A different view emphasizes the fact that this word "is used in the Greek translation of the Old Testament to translate the phrase *Mercy Seat*. In Hebrew ritual, the high priest appeared before the Ark of the Covenant, which contained the stone tablets of the Law. The priest sprinkled blood from a sacrifice on the golden lid of the Ark, which was called the Mercy Seat. The symbolism richly portrayed the fact that a broken law stood between God and the people, but through the shedding of blood, the place of judgment and estrangement became the place of mercy and reconciliation. Christ's death is therefore seen as the means whereby God's demand for justice against a sinful race is fully met, thereby freeing God to be merciful to those who formally merited only judgment." (See D. Stuart Briscoe, *The Communicator's Commentary, Romans;* pp. 93-94.)

Now, a picture from the human scene that will help us understand this magnificent truth: one of the most beautiful and moving love stories I have ever heard is that of Thomas Moore, the nineteenth-century Irish poet. Shortly after his marriage, he was called away on business. It was some time before he returned home, and when he did, he found waiting for him at the front door of the house, not his beautiful bride, but the family doctor.

"Your wife is upstairs," said the doctor, "but she's asked that you do not come up." Then Thomas Moore learned the terrible truth: his wife had contracted smallpox. The disease had left her once-flawless skin pocked and scarred. She had taken one look at her reflection in the mirror and had commanded the shutters be drawn and that her husband never see her again.

Moore would not listen. He ran upstairs and opened the door to his wife's room. It was black as night inside. Not a sound came from the darkness. Groping along the wall, Moore grasped for the gas jets.

A startled cry came from the black corner of the room. "No! Don't light the lamps!"

Moore hesitated, swayed by the pleading in the voice. "Go!" she begged, "Please go! This is the greatest gift I can give you now."

Moore did go. He went down to his study where he sat up most of the night, prayerfully writing—not a poem this time, but a song. He had never written a song before, but now it seemed more in keeping with his mood than simply poetry. He not only wrote the words, he wrote the music too. The next morning as soon as the sun was up, he returned to his wife's room. He felt his way to a chair and sat down. "Are you awake?" he asked.

"I am," came a voice from the far side of the room. "But you must not ask to see me. You must not press me, Thomas."

"I will sing to you, then," he answered. And so for the first time, Thomas Moore sang to his wife the song that still lives today:

> Believe me, if all those endearing young charms,
> which I gaze on so fondly today,
> Were to change by tomorrow and flee from my arms,
> like fairy gifts fading away,
> Thou wouldst still be adored, as this moment thou art,
> Let thy loveliness fade as it will . . .

He heard a movement from the dark corner where his wife lay in her loneliness, waiting. He continued:

Let thy loveliness fade as it will,
and round the dear ruin each wish of my heart
Would entwine itself verdantly still.

The song ended. As his voice trailed off the last note, Moore heard his bride arise. She crossed the room to the window, reached up, and slowly drew open the shutters. That's the power of love. And that is only a hint of the love of Christ for us.

We don't deserve that love. We can't earn it. It is given. Ravaged by the guilt and fear that result from this dreadful disease, pocked and scarred as we are by sin, we hear the love song of God: "Indeed, God did not send the Son into the world to condemn the world, but in order that the world might be saved through him" (John 3:17). We see that music translated into the sacrificial action of Christ on the cross. To this place of extravagant love and mercy we come. Believing that Christ died for us, miraculously the shutters are opened upon our dark world of sin, guilt, and fear. Our lives are flooded with the light of God's salvation, and God makes us "alive together with Christ," forever freed from the bondage of sin.

That is the keystone of Wesley's doctrine—salvation by faith—and it is all rooted in God's grace, which is the theme of our next chapter.

QUESTIONS FOR PERSONAL REFLECTION

1. For John Wesley, the goal of "getting to heaven" was a matter of highest priority (p. 2). List four or five goals of your life. Then, as you begin this study, honestly describe where the goal of "getting to heaven" fits into your overall goals.

2. On p. 4 is a set of questions that help illustrate the universality of sin and the need for salvation. Answer each of these questions specifically. What do your answers tell you about your own need for salvation?

3. Spend some time reflecting on your life. Are there more glaring or destructive "sins" than the ones listed in the questions?

4. In your own words, describe what it means to say that we are *saved by faith*.

5. Christ saves us from the *guilt* of sin (p. 5). Is there a burden of guilt in your life for which you have not accepted Christ's forgiveness? Write a brief description of any burden that you can identify.

If you are still struggling with guilt, consider sharing this with a trusted friend or pastor, asking for prayer for relief of the burden. Name the person(s) with whom you would be willing to share. Make plans to contact one of these persons immediately.

6. Salvation in Christ also saves us from two forms of fear: the fear of God's judgment (eternal punishment) and the fear that we might fall away from the grace of God (p. 7). Do you struggle with either of these forms of fear? Briefly describe these or any other fears that continue to challenge your faith.

7. The essence of the Wesleyan understanding of faith can be summed up in the statement: *In the cross, Christ did something for you that you can never do for yourself.* In your own words, describe what Christ did, and write a paragraph expressing your gratitude for Christ's work in your life.

QUESTIONS FOR GROUP SHARING

1. Discuss the notion of "getting to heaven" as a primary goal of life. Ask persons who are willing to share where this goal fits into their overall life goals.

2. Discuss what is meant by the universality of sin.

3. Invite as many persons as will to share their personal experiences of salvation from the *guilt*, the *fear*, or the *power* of sin.

4. Discuss the fact that salvation is a *present* reality, not simply a future hope.

5. Invite the group to respond to this statement: "In the cross, Christ did something for us that we can never do ourselves."

CHAPTER 2

AMAZING GRACE

"For God so loved the world that he gave his only Son, so that everyone who believes in him may not perish but may have eternal life. Indeed, God did not send the Son into the world to condemn the world, but in order that the world might be saved through him. Those who believe in him are not condemned; but those who do not believe are condemned already, because they have not believed in the name of the only Son of God. And this is the judgment, that the light has come into the world, and people loved darkness rather than light because their deeds were evil."
(John 3:16-19)

But now, apart from law, the righteousness of God has been disclosed, and is attested by the law and the prophets, the righteousness of God through faith in Jesus Christ for all who believe. For there is no distinction, since all have sinned and fall short of the glory of God; they are now justified by his grace as a gift, through the redemption that is in Christ Jesus, whom God put forward as a sacrifice of atonement by his blood, effective through faith. He did this to show his righteousness, because in his divine forbearance he had passed over the sins previously committed; it was to prove at the present time that he himself is righteous and that he justifies the one who has faith in Jesus. (Romans 3:21-26)

Computers and the Internet continue to amaze me. A friend used these amazing "tools" to send me an Easter message that was accompanied by about a dozen pictures of Jesus, each in sequence merging into and being transformed into the next. These were classic portraits by famous artists.

The series began with Mary and Joseph and the Baby Jesus, and continued to portray the sweep of Jesus' life: his baptism, teaching in the temple, instructing the fishermen for an unbelievable catch, the transfiguration, the last supper, Gethsemane, the Palm Sunday entry into Jerusalem, the cross, and the resurrection. It was a powerful reminder of the movement of Jesus' life, and especially meaningful as I was moving through Holy Week.

The movement of the Jesus story and the gospel was made more challenging by two other images from the newspaper that week. One was the picture of three children, playing at the site of a Holy Week tradition in San Fernando City, Philippines ("Place of Penitence—A Holy Week Tradition," Pat Roque, Associated Press, from *The Commercial Appeal*, Memphis, Tennessee, April 5, 2007). Three huge crosses dominated the scene where, as the caption noted, on Good Friday each year, some "devotee" of Christ will have himself nailed to the center cross to "imitate the suffering of Jesus." It happens every year in that predominantly Roman Catholic nation as Christians climax their Lenten season of penitence with a dramatic reenactment of the crucifixion.

A second photograph I saw that week was of four children accompanied by an adult. They were on their way to the new schoolhouse in Nickel Mines, Pennsylvania, that was built to replace the razed school where a gunman killed five Amish students and himself in October of 2006 (*The Commercial Appeal*, April 3, 2007).

How powerfully appropriate that this new school would reopen during Holy Week. I wondered if these Amish leaders planned it that way. We remember the awful story. A number of students and a few adults in a one-room Amish schoolhouse were taken hostage by a milk-truck driver, Charles Carl Roberts IV, on October 2, 2006. Several of the hostages were released, while a number of girls remained captive. The gunman shot eleven people, killing five of the girls, one girl was permanently disabled from a severe head wound, and we will never know the emotional damage done to the others.

What I remember most about the event were the parents of these little girls reaching out to the wife of the gunman, who had committed suicide after killing the victims. The parents extended compassion to Mrs. Roberts, assuring her that they forgave the man who imprisoned their children, murdering some, and maiming others; they even forgave him for intending to sexually molest these helpless little ones. They invited Mrs. Roberts to the funerals of their children, insisted that some of the money raised to help them be used to help her, and some of them even attended the graveside service of the man who had stolen their children from them.

Can you put those pictures together in your mind? The sweeping pictorial account of Jesus' life, the scene of a modern reenactment of the crucifixion, and a community of Christians who are dramatically living the meaning of the cross as they forgive the one who killed their daughters.

All the pictures converge into one . . . three crosses against a dark, stormy sky, with Jesus hanging on the center cross, struggling to speak that final word of grace, "Father, forgive them."

Grace—amazing grace: it is the heart of the Christian gospel. John captured it in this encompassing word: " 'For God so loved the world that he gave his only Son, so that everyone who believes in him may not perish but may have eternal life. Indeed, God did not send the Son into the world to condemn the world, but in order that the world might be saved through him' " (John 3:16-17).

And this is what Paul argued about so convincingly with the Romans: "Since all have sinned and fall short of the glory of God; they are now justified by his grace as a gift, through the redemption that is in Christ Jesus, whom God put forward as a sacrifice of atonement by his blood, effective through faith" (Romans 3:23-25).

John Wesley did us a great service and provided us with a distinctive emphasis by talking about grace impinging upon us and working in three specific ways: prevenient grace, justifying grace, and sanctifying grace. Prevenient grace is the grace of God going before us, pulling us, wooing us, seeking to open our minds and hearts, and eventually giving us faith. Justifying grace is the forgiving love of God, freely given to us, reconciling us, putting us right with God, making Christ, who knew no sin, to be sin on our behalf. Sanctifying grace is the work and spirit of Christ within us, restoring the broken image, completing the salvation that was begun in justification, and bringing us to complete newness of life and perfection in love.

We will discuss sanctifying grace in chapter 4. Here we will look at prevenient and justifying grace.

PREVENIENT GRACE

I have a picture in my office, a painting by my wife, Jerry. You have to study many paintings to get their meaning, and sometimes the meaning you get is not what the artist intended. I heard of a person who went into a museum of modern art. Looking around at what to him was a horrid onslaught of color and distorted design, he commented, "There is less here than meets the eye."

Now, my wife doesn't paint that way, but this piece is an impressionistic design of color and movement, dominantly blue, from deep shades to translucent light. The person in this painting, engulfed in the flow of color, is not obvious at first glance, but is distinct when really studied. The person stands in the swirl of color and movement surrounded by light and life that comes from somewhere beyond; yet you know it is this light and movement that is energizing and giving the person life.

Jerry called her painting "Grace" because it is the expression of her experience of God's love as proclaimed in the hymn "I Sought the Lord." At a particular time of struggle in her life, the hymn ministered to her, and her painting flowed from that experience.

> I sought the Lord, and afterward I knew
> He moved my soul to seek him, seeking me.
> It was not I that found, O Savior true;
> No, I was found of thee.
>
> Thou didst reach forth thy hand and mine enfold;
> I walked and sank not on the storm-vexed sea.
> 'Twas not so much that I on thee took hold,
> As thou, dear Lord, on me.
> (words Anonymous, ca. 1890; *The United Methodist Hymnal*, #341)

That's the nature of prevenient grace. The Lord seeks us before we begin to seek. Wesley sounded this note strongly in opposition to a doctrine of predestination. Whether the rigid, double predestination idea—that some are damned to hell while others are elected for heaven, or another variation on that theme—the doctrine of predestination has as its center an understanding of grace as limited. For Wesley—and this is another particularly Wesleyan emphasis—grace is universal. It is "free in all, and free for all." Bishop William R. Cannon makes the case:

> To be sure, it is free to all in the sense that it is given without price, that it does not demand anything of us before it is bestowed, and that it flows from the free mercy of God. But note the change. Grace is free *for all*. It is not free only for those whom God has ordained to life, but it is like the

> air we breathe, or the wind that blows in our faces; it is for everyone who dwells upon the face of the earth. (*The Theology of John Wesley*, p. 93)

Now, that doesn't mean that all persons receive this grace, or that they deliberately appropriate it, or respond to it for their salvation. They don't. That is the reason we began with the emphasis on faith in the first chapter. For salvation, we must respond in faith to God's grace. The truth is we receive prevenient grace before we can respond at all.

Prevenient grace (or "preventing grace") is the *grace that goes before.* Now, what does that mean? It means that before any conscious personal experience of divine grace, grace is there, working in our lives even before we are aware of it. The first move is God's, not ours. This is the witness of the scripture. As clear as anything else in the Bible is the fact that God seeks us. God is, as Francis Thompson would say, "the hound of heaven" who relentlessly pursues us. That's the story over and over again in the Bible—a searching God who takes the initiative in human life.

It all began with Adam and Eve in the garden. When they had sinned, they experienced guilt. They did not want to see God or for God to see them, so they hid. But God came looking for them, calling them by name, "Adam, Eve, where are you?"

Moses hid from God in Midian. He didn't want God to find him because he knew what God was going to ask him to do. The story goes on: Elijah hiding in a cave. Peter trying to hide his Galilean accent from those around the fire in the courtyard where Jesus stood trial.

That is the story: people hiding, God seeking. Jesus underscored it with the three parables Luke put together for "the gospel in the Gospel"—the parables of the lost coin, the lost sheep, and the lost son. That's the point of view of the Bible, what the scripture is all about—the story of God searching for us. Most of us thought it was the other way around, didn't we? We thought the Bible was the story about people who were looking for God. That really isn't so. It's the story of God seeking us.

So prevenient grace "goes before" us, preparing the soul for entrance into the initial state of salvation. As H. Orton Wiley says, "It is the preparatory grace of the Holy Spirit exercised toward man helpless in sin. As it respects the guilty, it may be considered mercy; as it respects the impotent, it is enabling power. It may be defined, therefore, as that manifestation of the divine influence which precedes the full regenerated life" (*Christian Theology*, Beacon Hill, 1941; 2:346).

In his underscoring of prevenient grace, Wesley echoed Peter's word that God is "not wanting any to perish, but all to come to repentance" (2 Peter 3:9).

Prevenient grace is not only "the grace that comes before," meaning that God takes the first step in our redemption; it is a *leading grace*. It is the activity of the Spirit in our lives, moving us to a place of repentance and reconciliation.

Many Wesleyan scholars talk of convicting or convincing grace as a distinct expression of grace. I see the dynamic as an expression of prevenient grace. Wesley includes the convicting and convincing dynamic in noting three ways in which prevenient grace leads us. One, it creates in us our first sensitivity to God's call, to God's seeking us, to God's will. Two, it produces an awareness and conviction that we have violated God's will and are not responsive to the divine call. Now, this conviction may be slight and transient, but it is real and is a part of God's prevenient grace working in us. And three, prevenient grace stimulates our first wish to please God.

These three workings of prevenient grace in our lives, according to Wesley, lead us to repentance, which is a necessary step to salvation. It is important to underscore what we noted earlier. God's grace is universal, but prevenient grace is not sufficient for salvation. A person may suppress or ignore this grace. If so, scripture warns that we may experience hardness of heart, so that these stirrings of the Spirit within will go unheeded. We will look at this again when we discuss free will and predestination in the next chapter.

Review a bit. Wesley said grace is "free in all, and free for all." No one is excluded from the work of prevenient grace. Grace is *for all*, a gift from God. But prevenient grace must be responded to in order for us to experience its justifying power. Through prevenient grace we are prompted and persuaded to respond to God's offer of salvation, but the free will granted by grace is not violated or overwhelmed by grace. Adam Clarke expresses it in this succinct fashion: "God gives the power (to believe), man uses the power thus given and brings glory to God: without the power, no man can believe; with it, any man can" (quoted by Roger E. Olson, *Arminian Theology*, IVP, 2006; p. 175).

JUSTIFYING GRACE

The resounding word of the New Testament is that we are justified by grace. That's good news!

Have you heard the story of the man who came home one night feeling very sorry for himself? Nothing had gone right at the office. It was one of those days when there seemed to be one hassle after another. When he arrived home, he could tell by the look on his wife's face that she had probably had the same kind of day. Before she could say anything, he said, "I don't know what your day has been like, and I don't know what you're getting ready to tell me, but if it's bad news, please keep it to yourself. I've had all the bad news I can stand for one day."

She looked at him with some uncertainty, and then said, "Well, maybe it is good news. You know we have six wonderful children." He said, "That's right." Then she said, "You'll be happy to know that five of them did not break an arm today."

Good news or bad news is sometimes a matter of perspective. The bad news of our life is that we have all sinned and fallen short of the glory of God. The good news is that God is gracious, and while we deserve condemnation, we are justified. God delivers us. We are saved by grace.

Justification is the common word used to describe what God does freely for us through grace. It is a metaphor primarily from the law courts. Keep in mind the supreme question: How can we as sinners get into a right relationship with God? How are we able to feel at peace, at ease, at home, with God? How can we escape the feeling of fear in the presence of God—the sense of estrangement, of judgment? That's the problem. Judaism answered the questions this way: a person can attain a right relationship with God by keeping the law. By fulfilling all the works of the law, a person will be right with God. But condemnation is implicit in this, for no one can live in perfect obedience, keeping every law. So salvation is not a way of works, but a way of faith.

Justification is based on the imagery of being on trial before God. *Diakioun* is the Greek word translated "to justify." William Barclay provides helpful insight into this word. All Greek verbs that end in *-oun* mean not to *make* someone something, but to *treat,* to *reckon,* or to *account* someone as something. The point about God's relationship to us is this: when we appear before God, we are anything but innocent; we are utterly guilty. Yet God *treats* us, *reckons* us, *and accounts* us as if we were innocent. That is what justification means.

When Paul says that God "justifies the ungodly" (Romans 4:5), he means that God, in incredible mercy, treats us as if we were godly people. This is what shocked the Jews. To treat a bad man as if he were a good man was the sign of a wicked judge. "He that justifieth the wicked, and he that condemneth the just, even they both are abomination to the LORD" (Proverbs 17:15 KJV). "I will not justify the wicked" (Exodus 23:7 KJV). But Paul says that is precisely what God does. (See William Barclay, *The Daily Study Bible: The Letter to the Romans;* p. 54.)

Though justification is a metaphor of the law court, we cannot understand the grace of God justifying us unless we see sin, not as a crime against law, but as a crime against love. To be sure, in sin we break God's law, but more important, we break God's heart. We may atone for a broken law, but how do we atone for a broken heart?

We have a painting in our breakfast room that would not be considered great art, but it is one that has profound meaning for us. It was painted by a friend who was a member of one of our former congregations. The painting is of a little black girl with haunting eyes that reflect a mixture of sadness and hope. Mary Jo, the artist, started painting as therapy for the deep sorrow of her life. This was one of her first paintings.

One afternoon, Mary Jo and her three daughters were at the shopping center, which was within walking distance of their home. She was carrying the baby, and the other two little blonde, blue-eyed girls were walking along where they should have been—ahead of her on the sidewalk. It happened without warning. An elderly man coming out of a parking place bumped another car, panicked, and hit the gas pedal instead of the brake. The car jumped the curb, crashed into one of the little girls, and threw her through the guardrail along the sidewalk and into a ravine below. She was dead—before her mother's eyes.

I don't know what happened to the driver. Drivers whose carelessness or recklessness takes lives are usually arrested, tried, found guilty, fined, sometimes imprisoned, their driver's license suspended. But after such persons have paid their fines or served their sentences, the law has no further claim upon them. As far as the law is concerned, justice has been served. The matter is over.

But that doesn't touch the issue of the parents' hearts whose child has been killed, or the heart of the driver himself. The driver of the car that snuffed out the life of our little friend could never make things up to her parents, never put things right by serving a sentence or paying a fine. Love—parental love—had ended in a heartbreak for all, and only the forgiveness of the little girl's parents could mend the relationship between them and the driver.

That is the way it is in our relationship with God. We may have broken God's laws, but the terrible tragedy is that we've broken God's heart.

Only an act of the free forgiveness of God's grace can bring us back into relationship with God. And that's what the cross is all about—*amazing grace*, justifying us.

I think about that amazing grace when I look at Mary Jo's painting. She forgave the man who killed her child and worked out her grief by painting the likeness of little children from all over the world. The little black girl in our breakfast room is one of those children. As I look into her sad but hopeful eyes, I am reminded that God is saddened by our sinfulness, but hopeful—always hopeful that none of us will perish but that all of us will come to repentance.

There is so much at the heart of what we Methodists/Wesleyans believe to be the core of the gospel and Christian experience that we need to look longer at this justifying aspect of grace. We do so by focusing on Paul's word: "Since all have sinned and fall short of the glory of God; they are now justified by his grace as a gift, through the redemption that is in Christ Jesus, whom God put forward as a sacrifice of atonement by his blood, effective through faith" (Romans 3:23-25).

Paul uses three metaphors in this passage that help us understand justifying grace. The first is *justification*, the metaphor from the law courts that we have already discussed. Before God's court, we are utterly guilty. Yet, in amazing mercy, God *treats* us, *reckons* us, *and accounts* us as innocent. When we believe that God loves us and that Christ died for us, and when we trust God's loving activity in Jesus Christ for our salvation, we are justified.

That leads to the second metaphor, that of *sacrifice*. Paul says God put forward Jesus Christ as a propitiation (or expiation) for our sin. The Greek word translated as *propitiation* or *expiation* has to do with sacrifice. This was prominent in the Old Testament, but it was also present in most religions. To appease God, sacrifices were offered. These were efforts to avert the wrath of God. The pattern in the Old Testament was the offering of animal sacrifices. But even in the Old Testament, there are the stirrings that such were not adequate. David stated it clearly out of the anguish of his own sin and guilt: "For you have no delight in sacrifice; / if I were to give a burnt offering, you would not be pleased. / The sacrifice acceptable to God is a broken spirit; / a broken and contrite heart, O God, you will not despise" (Psalm 51:16-17). Likewise, Micah made the case: "'With what shall I come before the LORD, / and bow myself before God on high? / Shall I come before him with burnt offerings, / with calves a year old? / Will the LORD be pleased with thousands of rams, with ten thousands of rivers of oil? / Shall I give my firstborn for my transgression, / the fruit of my body for the sin of my soul?' " (Micah 6:6-7).

Paul concluded that only one sacrifice was sufficient—the sacrifice Jesus made on the cross. That sacrifice alone can atone and open the door to God that no other effort or action can accomplish.

The third metaphor Paul uses is taken from slavery. He speaks of the redemption, or deliverance, which is in Christ Jesus. The Greek word is *apolutrōsis,* which means a ransoming, a redeeming, and a liberating. It means that we are in the power, the grip, the dominion of sin; Christ alone can free us.

There are all sorts of images for this. Among Christians in one section of Africa, the New Testament word for redemption means "God took our heads out." It's a strange phrase, but when you trace it back to the nineteenth century, when slave trading was practiced, the meanings become powerful.

White men invaded African villages and carried men, women, and children off into slavery. Each slave had an iron collar buckled around his or her neck, and the collar was attached to a chain. That chain was attached to the iron collar around the neck of another, and another, until there would be a long chain of slaves, driven to the coast and shipped off to England or the United States.

From time to time, as the chain of slaves made its way to the coast, a relative, a loved one, or a friend would recognize someone who had been captured and would offer a ransom to remove the collar and free the person. Thus the word for redemption: "God took our heads out."

However we state it, whatever image we use out of our own cultures, the word *redemption* means that God's action in Jesus Christ sets us free from the bondage of sin, guilt, and death. No single image is adequate. All images together do not probe the depth of the mystery. It is the mystery of what God does for us in Jesus Christ that we cannot do ourselves. It is justifying us when we are utterly guilty, providing a sacrifice when we have nothing to offer, and setting us free when we are powerless to break the strong tentacles of sin. Wesley provides a good summary of it:

> This then is the salvation which is through faith, even in the present world: a salvation from sin, and the consequences of sin, both often expressed in the word *justification;* which, taken in the largest sense, implies a deliverance from guilt and punishment, by the atonement of Christ actually applied to the soul of the sinner now believing on Him, and a deliverance from the (whole body) of sin, through Christ *formed*

> *in his heart*. So, that he who is thus justified, or saved by faith, is indeed *born again*. He is *born again of the Spirit* into a new life, which "is hid with Christ in God." (He is a new creature: old things are passed away: all things in him are become new.) And as a newborn babe, he gladly receives the . . . "*sincere* milk of the word, and grows thereby"; going on in the might of the Lord his God, from faith to faith, from grace to grace, until at length, he comes unto "a perfect man, unto the measure of the stature of the fullness of Christ." (*Fifty-Three Sermons*, p. 23)

When you ponder a passage such as this, you understand why some Wesley scholars prefer to use the term "converting" rather than "justifying" grace. They rightly note that both justification (what God does for us) and regeneration (what God does in us) are held together in the designation "converting grace."

We will consider this at greater length in the next chapter as we look specifically at the power of sin in our lives, the sin from which we are freed. Then, in chapter 4 we will return to Wesley's theme song, *grace*, as we consider sanctifying grace, or Christian perfection.

QUESTIONS FOR PERSONAL REFLECTION

1. Recall your most vivid experience of forgiveness—of being forgiven or of forgiving another. Write enough about that experience to relive it in your mind.

2. Recall an example of God's prevenient grace in your life—the knowledge, in retrospect, that God was seeking you or leading you before you were aware of or had acknowledged God's grace (p. 21). Make enough notes to get the experience clearly in mind.

3. Can you recall when you became aware of the fact that God's grace is "free in all, and free for all"?

4. Sin is not simply a crime against law; it is a crime against love (p. 24). Can you recall a personal experience, your own or someone else's, where a "crime against love" was forgiven? Describe that experience.

5. The apostle Paul used three metaphors to describe the meaning and significance of our justification in Christ—(1) being reckoned innocent in a court of law, (2) being reconciled through sacrifice, and (3) being set free from slavery (pp. 25–26). Which of these is most descriptive of your own experience of justification? Why?

QUESTIONS FOR GROUP SHARING

1. Invite two or three persons to share their most vivid experiences of being forgiven or of forgiving another.

2. Invite two or three persons to share how prevenient grace has worked specifically in their lives.

3. Discuss Wesley's idea of *universal grace* in light of Bishop Cannon's descriptive phrase, "free in all, free for all."

4. Discuss what difference it makes to see sin as a crime against love, rather than simply as a crime against law.

5. Invite persons to share their experiences of justification in terms of the three metaphors that Paul uses. Are all three metaphors represented in the group's experiences?

CHAPTER 3

SIN: THERE'S NOTHING ORIGINAL ABOUT IT!

Did that which is good, then, bring death to me? By no means! It was sin, working death in me through what is good, in order that sin might be shown to be sin, and through the commandment might become sinful beyond measure. For we know that the law is spiritual; but I am of the flesh, sold into slavery under sin. I do not understand my own actions. For I do not do what I want, but I do the very thing I hate. Now if I do what I do not want, I agree that the law is good. But in fact it is no longer I that do it, but sin that dwells within me. For I know that nothing good dwells within me, that is, in my flesh. I can will what is right, but I cannot do it. For I do not do the good I want, but the evil I do not want is what I do. Now if I do what I do not want, it is no longer I that do it, but sin that dwells within me. So I find it to be a law that when I want to do what is good, evil lies close at hand. For I delight in the law of God in my inmost self, but I see in my members another law at war with the law of my mind, making me captive to the law of sin that dwells in my members. Wretched man that I am! Who will rescue me from this body of death? Thanks be to God through Jesus Christ our Lord! So then, with my mind I am a slave to the law of God, but with my flesh I am a slave to the law of sin. There is therefore now no condemnation for those who are in Christ Jesus. For the law of the Spirit of life in Christ Jesus has set you free from the law of sin and of death. (Romans 7:13–8:2)

Somewhere along the way I heard of a little Christian college in Arkansas that advertised in its bulletin that it was sixteen miles from any known sin.

Now, I grew up in the backwoods of Mississippi, and I know that Arkansas and Mississippi are a lot alike. But nowhere in my backwoods Mississippi could you get six miles, much less sixteen, from any known sin. Sin is not in a place, and you can't get away from it. Sin is in the person.

In this chapter we will look at the root of all human problems. The great majority of theologians talk about original sin. The fact is, there's nothing original about sin!

Think about that for a moment: there's nothing original about sin. What is the worst thing you've ever done in your life? Or, what have you done in the past month that you would label sinful? What led you to do that? Do you think you are the first person ever to act, feel, or relate in the fashion you are labeling sinful? There's nothing *original* about sin.

Augustine is one of the premier theologians of all times. In his classic book, *Confessions*, he told the story of his youthful escapades of stealing pears from a neighbor's tree. He recorded that late one night a group of youngsters went out to "shake down and rob this tree." They took great loads of fruit from it, "not for our own eating but rather to throw to the pigs." Augustine went on to berate himself for the depth of sin this revealed: "The fruit gathered, I threw away, devouring in it only iniquity. There was no other reason, but foul was the evil, and I loved it."

Now, why would one harmless prank such as this loom so large in Augustine's mind? By his own admission, he had taken a mistress, fathered a child out of wedlock, and indulged in every fleshly passion. Surely any of these was more serious than stealing pears.

Augustine saw in the "pear incident" his true nature and the nature of all humankind: in each of us there is sin. Some would soften this and say that within each of us there is the *susceptibility* to sin. But Wesley, in the train of Paul and Augustine, would say sin is there—not just a proneness to it, but sin itself. Since Adam, sin has been a part of every human life.

In this chapter, we will deal with the question of "original sin." But also, in light of the preceding chapters on salvation by faith, and prevenient and justifying grace, we will look at two other core concerns of a United Methodist Christian: predestination and freedom, and regeneration and the new birth.

SIN IS UNIVERSAL

John Wesley talked more about the *universality* of sin than he did about "original sin." I think he did this because he was not willing to go as far as Augustine, for instance, on the total depravity of human nature. But he wasn't far from that position. He believed in "total depravity," but as Gilbert Rowe put it, not in "teetotal depravity." This was so because of Wesley's emphasis on grace. That's the reason we dealt with grace in the preceding chapter. But let's be clear. Apart from grace, expressed "preveniently," as Wesley would say, the natural person is utterly corrupted.

Recall that we said grace is universal, not limited. In Wesley's word, grace is "free in all, and free for all." About that there was no question. Wesley was as pessimistic about human nature as one could be, but there was a kind of optimism in his pessimism. Wesley scholar Robert Tuttle says that "original righteousness" precedes original sin in Wesleyan theology. He describes it as "good news, bad news, good news"—the good news of creation, the bad news of the fall, and the good news of redemption.

Somewhere I saw a cartoon of a man sitting on a park bench; his clothes were tattered and torn, his toes were coming out of his shoes—the stereotypical hobo. Beneath the picture was the caption: "No man is completely worthless—he can always serve as a horrible example." Wesley knew himself and all human beings to be sinners, and we need to come to grips with that. But—and this is the rhythm and balance that is unique to Wesleyan theology—he was optimistic about grace. God's grace is sufficient. The power of sin is overcome by the power of God's love, mercy, and forgiveness. So John Wesley would join in the joyful, triumphant cry of the apostle Paul: "Where sin increased, grace abounded all the more" (Romans 5:20). Because of prevenient grace, universally bestowed by God, our freedom to respond to God is always guaranteed. We'll come back to this in a moment; for now, return to sin. (Now, I don't mean that literally, though that is the human pattern; we're constantly returning to sin!)

Have you read about the small town of Centralia, Pennsylvania? It's a mining town. Several decades ago, a fire broke out in the labyrinthine maze of tunnels and shafts that honeycomb the earth beneath the town. First the local, then the state, and then federal mine officials tried to put the fire out. They have done everything they know, but it just keeps burning. Now and then a puff of smoke will break through the surface just to let everyone know the fire is still there.

Sin is like that. It is not always rampant in our lives, though it often is. It's there—and there's nothing original about it.

The text for Wesley's sermon on original sin was Genesis 6:5: "The LORD saw that the wickedness of humankind was great in the earth, and that every inclination of the thoughts of their hearts was only evil continually." Wesley laid the foundation for his sermon on original sin by sweeping quotations from scripture.

> The scripture avers, that "by one man's disobedience all men were constituted sinners"; that "in Adam, all died," spiritually died, lost the life and image of God; that fallen, sinful Adam then "begat a son in his own likeness"—nor was it possible he should beget him in any other; for "who can bring a clean thing out of unclean?" — That consequently we, as well as other men, were by nature "dead in trespasses and sin, without hope, without God in the world," and, therefore, "children of wrath"; that every man may say, "I was shaped in wickedness, and in sin did my mother conceive me"; that "there is no difference," in that "all have sinned and come short of the glory of God," of that glorious image of God wherein man was originally created. And hence, when the Lord looked down from heaven upon the children of men, He saw they were all gone out of the way; that they were altogether become abominable, there was none righteous, no, not one, "none that truly sought after God." (*Fifty-Three Sermons;* p. 558)

The scripture passage with which we began this chapter is no isolated word from Paul. It is the witness of scripture that with anguish Paul pours out in a personal confession. Is there a more poignant expression of the civil war raging within? "For I know that nothing good dwells within me, that is, in my flesh. I can will what is right, but I cannot do it.... Wretched man that I am! Who will rescue me from this body of death?" (Romans 7:18-20, 24). What a raging fire of conscience! What a gripping heart cry! How often do we feel that ripping inside, the tearing apart of our efforts to be whole and centered and headed in a clear direction!

It is not only a personal problem; it happens in the whole of society. During World War I, Karl Barth was the pastor of a village church in Switzerland. A great darkness had descended upon Europe. Seemingly all the lights had gone out. Barth's people were crying for some word from the Lord that would make sense out of what had happened. Barth, however, had been raised in the nineteenth century and trained in its optimistic humanism, therefore he had nothing to preach. In desperation he turned to the scripture and discovered what he called "the strange new world within the Bible." Out of that experience, he wrote a book entitled *The Word of God and the Word of Man*. What Barth found in the Bible was strange because it described a world unlike the image of the world held by the confident liberals of the nineteenth century. When he came to Paul's letter to the Romans, Barth found there a diagnosis of the human condition that offered a reason for the chaos of his time.

The beginning point for Paul is stark realism about sin. He rejects, out of hand, the idea that sin is something we can get rid of with proper upbringing, or good education, or healthy environment, or evolutionary development, or cultural growth and planned development of civilization. Sin is at the very heart of our lives—in fact, sin lies beneath the surface of our lives and penetrates to the very core. That's what we mean when we talk about original sin. And there's nothing original about it because we are all infected by it.

So don't be naive about sin in your life, Paul would say—and likewise, Wesley and the early Methodists. The Duchess of Buckingham complained to the Countess of Huntingdon about this radical doctrine of sin being preached by the early Methodist preachers and received this reply from the countess: "I thank your Ladyship for the information concerning the Methodist preachers. Their doctrines are most repulsive and strongly tinctured with impertinence and disrespect toward their superiors, in perpetually endeavoring to level all ranks and do away with all distinctions. It is monstrous to be told that you have a heart as sinful as the common wretches that crawl the earth" (W. E. H. Lecky, *A History of England in the 18th Century*, New Edition [London: Longmans, Green & Company, 1892], III; p. 122).

There are those in our day who still think it impertinent and repulsive to talk about sin in this fashion. For them, the problems of society and personal misery are located not in our alienation from God—not in our sin—but somewhere else. Our ignorance, not sin, is the problem. Psychological maladjustment, not sin, is our dilemma. Our surroundings are what "get to us"—not sin. Our feeling of powerlessness—not sin—that's the reason we're so impotent in living effectively in the world. Our economic inequities, our limited education, the inequality among persons—not sin—that's what is driving this country mad. So if we improve education, if we cultivate self-understanding, if we raise everybody's standard of living, if we arrange proper socialization—then people will be saved and will be happy and fulfilled. Evil will disappear, and the problems of the world will be solved.

So we tend to want to leave sin to the rescue missions, to the fundamentalist sects, to TV evangelists. Sin doesn't fit in our enlightened age of self-actualization, social engineering, positive thinking, and the delusion of "I'm OK, You're OK."

I think Wesley would laugh at us. He insisted that belief in a doctrine of universal sin is "the first distinguishing point between heathenism and Christianity.... Is man by nature filled with all manner of evil? Is he void of all good? Is he wholly fallen? Is his soul totally corrupted?... Allow this and you are so far a Christian. Deny it and you are heathen still" (Albert Outler, *Theology in the Wesleyan Spirit*; p. 37).

Now, this is a grim picture, but the Gospels, the apostle Paul, and Wesley have a saving word for us. In his understanding of sin, Wesley took a position between the extreme of teetotal depravity—in which we are utterly and hopelessly sinful, the image of God within having been obliterated—and the naive contention that we are able to sin or not to sin as we choose.

Wesley condemned the latter, the notion that we are able to sin or not sin as we please. Scripture and experience argue convincingly against the possibility that we can banish sin from our lives and from society if we can simply muster up sufficient moral effort and courage.

But Wesley also refused to go to the other extreme of Calvin: that with the image of God within us obliterated, we are utterly and hopelessly sinful. Again, this is the reason Wesley's teaching about grace, especially prevenient grace, is so important. Apart from prevenient grace, the moral image is utterly destroyed. So instead of seeing sin as an obliteration of the image of God within us, he saw it as a *malignant disease* that could be cured only by the powerful grace of God. And this brings us to talk about predestination and free will.

PREDESTINATION OR FREEDOM?

The extreme diagnosis of the human condition—that we are teetotally depraved—has it that the image of God has been completely obliterated by Adam's fall. There is no way to change that. Thus comes the doctrine of *predestination* and *election*. Some are predestined to salvation by God's sovereign choice—and that is their only hope. For those who are not predestined to salvation—well, you know their fate.

Now, here is a unique Wesley nuance: Wesley contended that the image of God in persons was not obliterated by the Fall; it was distorted, broken, obscured, crusted over with sin and self-will, but not obliterated. Sin was a malignant disease always portending death, apart from the miracle of God's grace.

Then came the second big difference. Wesley's understanding of "prevenient grace" and free will displaced the notion of unconditional election. Methodists/Wesleyans embrace "conditional predestination" grounded in prevenient grace and based on God's foreknowledge of who will freely accept God's gracious offer of salvation.

Calvin said, "We shall never be clearly convinced as we ought to be, that our salvation flows from the fountain of God's free mercy, till we are acquainted with his eternal election, which illustrates the grace of God by this comparison, that he adopts not all promiscuously to the hope of salvation, but gives to some what he refuses to others" (John Calvin, *Institutes of the Christian Religion*, II, iii; p. 3).

For Calvin, predestination meant that God has determined once and for all, by immutable and eternal decree, all those who will be admitted to salvation and those who will be condemned to destruction. So for him, justifying grace was restricted, limited, and particular. But not so with Wesley.

At the heart of Wesley's proclamation of the gospel was God's offer of grace to all. God's love is for the whole world. Through God's prevenient grace, our free will to accept or resist God's grace is restored. So Wesley felt the doctrine of predestination was full of blasphemy. "Of such blasphemy," he says in his *Notes on the New Testament* (p. 489), "as I should dread to mention, but that the honor of our gracious God and the cause of truth will not suffer me to be silent."

He argued on the basis of reason and experience, but primarily on the basis of scripture. How can it be?

> This doctrine of predestination and election makes Jesus Christ a hypocrite, a deceiver of men, and a leader without honesty or ordinary sincerity. For it cannot be denied that Jesus everywhere speaks as if he is willing that all men should be saved. Listen to his pleas to the Jews in Matthew 23:37: "O Jerusalem, Jerusalem, killing the prophets and stoning those who are sent to you! How often would I have gathered your children together as a hen gathers her brood under her wings, and you would not!" His words are full of invitations to sinners: "Come to me, all who labor and are heavy laden, and I will give you rest" (Matt. 11:28). If you say that he did not intend to save all sinners, if you say he

> calls those that cannot come, then you represent the Son of God as mocking his helpless creatures by offering what he never intends to give. You describe him as saying one thing and meaning another; as pretending the love which he had not, "Him, in whose mouth was no guile," you make full deceit, void of common sincerity.
>
> ("Sermon CXXVIII," Section 24)

Wesley was vehemently opposed to a doctrine of predestination and election because he felt it affected the whole of Christian belief and experience. This is so crucial in the Wesleyan way of salvation that we have added a final chapter to this edition on the Methodist/Wesleyan response to Calvinism.

If we had to select a single gospel message to present the essence of God's intention for us, would it not be that text from John 3:16-17? "For God so loved the world that he gave his only Son, so that everyone who believes in him may not perish but have eternal life. Indeed, God did not send the Son into the world to condemn the world, but in order that the world might be saved through him." There's nothing exclusive or limited about that.

So we United Methodists contend with John Wesley that sin is universal, but that grace is free in all and free for all, that whosoever will, may come.

REGENERATION IS REQUIRED

Since sin is universal and is a malignant infection in our life, to use a medical image, radical surgery is essential to deal with it. *Regeneration* is required; a new birth. As stated in the last chapter, justification and regeneration are a part of "converting" grace. Not only are we forgiven, not only are we reconciled to God, we are made new, regenerated. This is what the psalmist was pleading for: "Create in me a clean heart, O God, / and put a new and right spirit within me" (Psalm 51:10). This is what Paul contended would happen to us: "If anyone is in Christ, there is a new creation: everything old has passed away; see, everything has become new!" (2 Corinthians 5:17).

Now, this requires radical surgery. And the radical surgery that will heal the malignant disease of sin involves a threefold prescription: one, repentance which flows from honest self-knowledge and includes genuine sorrow and remorse; two, renunciation of self-will, a willingness to yield our wills to Christ since our will is the seat of our sin; and three, faith, which is a complete trust in God's sheer, unmerited grace.

We are not helpless creatures, predestined to either eternal death or eternal life. We *are* free. We *do* participate in our salvation. We respond. When we finally come to ourselves and realize that we are sinners beyond hope of saving ourselves, that God's grace is for us, that God's unmerited love is not to be earned but to be received, we drop to our knees to receive our Redeemer in an embrace of faith and acceptance.

As all images and metaphors are limited, so talking about sin as a malignant disease needs some added word. The term may suggest no responsibility or accountability on our part. Not so. We are responsible and accountable for our sin, and "healing" is not adequate to describe our salvation. As indicated, regeneration—new birth—is required. More than a healing dynamic, this is a movement from death to life. (See Ephesians 2:1-10.)

Here is a hint of it in the story of Benjamin West, who tells us about how he became a painter. One day his mother went out, leaving him in charge of his little sister, Sally. He discovered some bottles of colored ink and began to paint Sally's portrait. He really made a mess of things. Ink blots were all over. On her return, the mother saw the mess, but grace prevailed. She said nothing, picked up one piece of paper, and saw the drawing. "It's Sally," she said immediately and excitedly, and then gave Benjamin a kiss. Later, this great painter, Benjamin West, said, "My mother's kiss made me a painter."

God's kiss of grace makes us Christian—an extravagant grace that works within us, preveniently, preserving that last bit of freedom that is ours to respond to, working as unmerited love to justify us and account us as righteous even though we are sinners—to *regenerate us*, to give us new birth—and finally sanctify us, making us new creatures. It is sanctifying grace that we will discuss in the next chapter.

Wesley closed his sermon on original sin with this word:

> Keep to the plain old faith, "once delivered to the saints," and delivered by the Spirit of God to our hearts. Know your disease! Know your cure! You were born to sin: therefore, "you must be born again," born of God. By nature ye are wholly corrupted: by grace ye shall be wholly renewed. In Adam, ye all died: in the second Adam, in Christ, ye all are made alive. "You that were dead in sins hath He quickened": he hath already given you a principle of life, even faith in Him who loved you and gave

> Himself for you! Now "go on from faith to faith," until your whole sickness be healed, and all that "mind be in you which was also in Christ Jesus"! (*Fifty-Three Sermons;* p. 566)

To that, I only add that, redeemed by Christ, we will continue to sing in awe:

> And can it be that I should gain
> An interest in the Savior's blood!
> Died he for me? who caused his pain!
> For me? who him to death pursued?
> Amazing love! How can it be
> That thou, my God, shouldst die for me?
> (Words by Charles Wesley, 1739; *The United Methodist Hymnal*, #363)

QUESTIONS FOR PERSONAL REFLECTION

1. Augustine recognized his bent to sin in the relatively harmless incident of stealing pears (p. 32). Looking back in your own life, is there an experience that witnesses to you the fact that in each of us there is sin?

2. Reflect on the fire that burns beneath the town of Centralia, Pennsylvania (p. 33). Do you experience recurring outbreaks of anger, greed, selfishness, possessiveness, lust, jealousy, and so on, that remind you of sin in your life?

3. Look at the immediate past week of your life. Has anything happened to remind you of the residual presence of sin in your life?

4. Read Romans 7:18-24. After pondering Paul's description, write a paragraph about your own struggle with sin. Write enough to express your feelings as clearly as possible.

5. Recall the last conversation you had with anyone about sin. What did that conversation reflect about how seriously we take the problem of sin?

6. Look at your life over the past month. What do your actions, attitudes, and relationships say about the contention that we are able to sin or not to sin as we choose?

7. Wesley's understanding of prevenient grace and free will displaced the Calvinist notions of predestination and election (pp. 36–38). Take some time to ponder this contrast. How does this challenge your thinking about God? About your relationship to God?

8. Read the paragraph on pp. 38–39 that begins, "Now, this requires radical surgery . . ." How have you responded to this threefold prescription? What part of it may not have been completed in your life?

Write your own prayer to God in response to this prescription.

QUESTIONS FOR GROUP SHARING

1. Invite two or three people to share their experiences in life that witness to the fact that *in each of* us *there is sin.*

2. Discuss why Wesley talked more about the *universality* of sin than about "original" sin (pp. 33–34).

3. Reflecting on the image of the fire burning beneath Centralia, Pennsylvania, share other images or experiences in your own life that illustrate the universality, the residual presence, of sin.

4. Discuss the following two questions:
   a) Is there within our culture and in the church an assumption that the ills of humankind can be overcome with proper education, healthy environment, and social caring about fundamental human needs, and political and social commitments to human good?
   b) What is the evidence in your community, and in our world, that this assumption about curing our human ills is true or false?

5. Discuss your personal beliefs and understandings, as well as what you have heard the church say, about sin as the source of human ills.

6. Look at the discussion you have just had in the light of Wesley's word that recognizing the reality of universal sin is "the first distinguishing point between heathenism and Christianity." (Read the entire statement on p. 36.)

7. Discuss the notion of predestination in terms of what it says about God's nature. Think about this in terms of God's *sovereignty*, the Calvinist's primary concern, and God's *universal grace and love*, the Wesleyan emphasis. How do we harmonize sovereignty and universal grace?

8. Ask if anyone would like to share her or his personal response to the threefold prescription for the healing of sin (no. 8 in "Questions for Personal Reflection").

CHAPTER 4

BUT NO ONE CAN BE PERFECT! WHO SAYS?

For this is the will of God, your sanctification: that you abstain from fornication. (1 Thessalonians 4:3)

For God did not call us to impurity but in holiness. (1 Thessalonians 4:7)

For I am the LORD who brought you up from the land of Egypt, to be your God; you shall be holy, for I am holy. (Leviticus 11:45)

Be perfect, therefore, as your heavenly Father is perfect. (Matthew 5:48)

Let those of us then who are mature be of the same mind; and if you think differently about anything, this too God will reveal to you. (Philippians 3:15)

For me to write a chapter on Christian perfection may appear to those who know me like the man who proposed to write a book with the title *Humility, and How I Attained It*. Even so, it must be done, for Wesley viewed Christian perfection as the *grand despositum* of Methodism.

We are returning to pick up Wesley's theme of grace. In chapter 2 we discussed *prevenient* and *justifying* grace. Now to complete the trilogy: *sanctifying* grace. Our attention may be riveted on the theme by thinking about perfection, for that is what sanctifying grace is all about: Christian perfection. Thus the title of this chapter: "*But No One Can Be Perfect!* Who Says?"

Wesley believed that God had raised up the people called Methodist to keep asking the question "Who says?"—and to do this by claiming and proclaiming the scriptural call to holiness of heart and life.

We could have chosen any number of scripture passages to undergird this chapter, for the Bible is full of injunctions to perfection, to purity of heart and life—to holiness. God put the call clearly in Leviticus 11:45: "Be holy, because I am holy" (NIV). And Jesus put it as clearly in his Sermon on the Mount: "Be perfect, therefore, as your heavenly Father is perfect" (Matthew 5:48). Wesley said it this way: "Ye know that the great end of religion is, to renew our hearts in the image of God, to repair this total loss of righteousness and true holiness which we sustained by the sin of our first parents" (John Wesley, "Original Sin", Sermon 44, section III.5, text from the 1872 edition, Thomas Jackson, editor; full text located at The United Methodist General Board of Global Ministries website: http://new.gbgm-umc.org/umhistory/wesley/sermons/44/).

Interestingly, Wesley chose Philippians 3:12 for the text of his basic sermon on Christian perfection. You remember this verse as Paul's word about his own life: "Not that I have already obtained this or am already perfect" (RSV).

Now, that may seem to be an argument against perfection, but in his introduction to the sermon, Wesley reminded his hearers and readers that immediately after Paul's disclaimer, he made a specific claim in verse 15: "Let us, therefore," he said, "as many as be perfect, be thus minded" (KJV). This seeming conflict in the claim of Paul is a clear call to seek understanding of what we mean when we talk about sanctification, holiness, or Christian perfection. All three words point to the same work of grace in our lives—sanctifying grace.

Let us then seek clarity about the meaning of sanctification, this central United Methodist doctrine. To do so, we must review a bit. To picture the idea of salvation, Wesley used the interesting image of a house. Repentance was the porch; justification was the entry-door; and all the rooms in the house were facets of our sanctification. It all begins with repentance—when we are convinced and convicted of our sins, are genuinely sorry, and accept by faith what God has done for us in Jesus Christ. When we respond in faith to God's grace, we are justified, made right with God, not because of our merit, but by divine grace. *Justification* is another word for pardon. So justification is what God does *for* us. And now the big issue, our focus: *Sanctification is what God does in us,* a work begun with regeneration and the new birth. As Albert Outler would remind us: "In justification we *gain* God's favor; holy-living is the life-process in which we seek to *retain* it [that favor]" (*Theology in the Wesleyan Spirit;* p. 57).

It will help us to realize that salvation, then, is a process—a process that begins with justification but continues as we grow in grace toward sanctification, which is the goal of our salvation. Sanctifying grace is the work of Christ within us—Christ's spirit restoring the broken image, completing what was begun in justification.

A tragedy occurred in the Wesleyan tradition in the nineteenth century, moving this doctrine of sanctification from the mainstream into an eddy that has been stirred only now and then in the mainline Methodist movement. A revival of emphasis on holiness began to move through the church. As is so often the case, people began to preach a particularized experience as the norm. Doctrines were clearly and rigidly defined. A big segment of the church objected strenuously to particular ideas about holiness, and especially rejected a notion of "second blessing sanctification." At the risk of oversimplification, the doctrine of "second blessing sanctification" claimed that in a second experience of grace, like that operative in conversion or justification, a person might have his or her carnal nature eradicated so that one could live a sinless life. Unfortunately, for some the doctrine was cast in concrete, rigidly and tenaciously presented as the standard for Christian living.

We fail to do justice to Wesley if we do not recognize that in his growth and teaching he changed. Though he initially thought he was "entirely" sanctified at Aldersgate, he changed his thinking and feeling about the matter. We do not give Wesley's hallmark doctrine of sanctification its full due unless we see it as a dynamic, not a static, thing. We may look at it in this fashion: the new birth is our initial sanctification; Christian perfection is entire sanctification.

Sanctification, then, comes both in a moment and as a lifelong process. We are born into sanctification (by grace); then we grow in it by grace. Sin remains a problem. Wesley preached sermons on sin and repentance in believers; yet he clearly stated that many of those who are sanctified are no longer tempted.

So just as tragic as casting the doctrine too narrowly and rigidly was the reaction of many who, failing to be able to harmonize the proclamation about perfection and holiness with experienced reality, threw the baby out with the bathwater. Rejecting an altogether too narrow definition of sanctification or holiness, and fleeing from an obvious stance of self-righteousness, they went to the opposite extreme and forgot sanctification altogether. For some time, little attention has been given to "holiness," especially within the mainstream of United Methodism.

Yet no reputable Wesleyan scholar denies that this was one of Wesley's foremost contributions to an understanding of the Christian gospel and the Christian way. *So*, let's take a solid look at it.

With the Wesleyan family's varying emphasis on the different aspects of sanctification, it is helpful to keep in mind Wesley's *order of sanctification*. He taught that sanctification is a process/moment/process. Some will argue, with good support from Wesley, that entire sanctification is the beginning point of the process. But that does not preclude a process of spiritual growth preceding the *moment* of entire sanctification. Wesley's understanding of grace assumed that there could be such a moment. For, if God sanctifies a believer—and God does—then God can do it in a moment. Even so, as prevenient grace leads a person to justification, sanctifying grace leads to the moment of entire sanctification. Then the process continues: process/moment/process.

To get a clearer understanding of this, let's consider (1) what Christian perfection is not, (2) what Christian perfection is, and (3) what sanctifying grace does in our lives.

PERFECTION IS NOT...

First, what Christian perfection is not.

Christian perfection is not freedom from ignorance. The Bible and Wesley are very clear about this: sanctifying grace does not turn us into superhuman robots, computerized and controlled by God to think and perform in all-knowing ways. No, we will always be limited in our wisdom and understanding. We will always "see through a glass darkly"—until that happy day in the kingdom when the scales will be removed from our eyes, and we will see clearly and know even as we are known.

If Christian perfection means that we will never in this life be free of ignorance and lack of understanding, it certainly follows that *we will neither be free of error or mistake*. John Wesley put a proviso on this one. He said, "It is true, the children of God do not mistake as to the things essential to salvation: they do not 'put darkness for light, or light for darkness': neither 'seek death in the error of their life.' For they are 'taught of God'; and the way which he teaches them, the way of holiness, is so plain, that 'the wayfaring man, though a fool, need not err therein.' But in things unessential to salvation they do err, and that frequently" ("Christian Perfection," Sermon 40, section I.4: http://new.gbgm-umc.org/umhistory/wesley/sermons/40/).

Wesley wanted to leave no excuse for the superficial notion that we do not know enough to be saved, or that we do not know enough to live a holy life.

I'm especially impressed by what Wesley said about interpretation of scripture, for this has been the cause for schism in the church throughout our history. Listen to him: "Nay, with regard to the holy Scriptures themselves, as careful as they are to avoid it, the best of men are liable to mistake, and do mistake day by day; especially with respect to those parts thereof which less immediately relate to practice. Hence, even the children of God are not agreed as to the interpretation of many places in holy writ; nor is their difference of opinion any proof that they are not the children of God on either side; but it is a proof that we are no more to expect any living man to be infallible than to be omniscient" (Sermon 40, section I.5, Ibid.).

The third thing Christian perfection is not is *freedom from infirmities*. Again, we need to be clear about the meaning. By infirmities Wesley was not giving anyone an out to sin—in fact he warned against giving this "soft title to known sins." Let Wesley state his own conviction on this matter:

> So, one man tells us, "Every man has his infirmity, and mine is drunkenness"; another has the infirmity of uncleanness; another, that of taking God's holy name in vain; and yet another has the infirmity of calling his brother, "Thou fool" or returning "railing for railing." It is plain that all you who thus speak, if ye repent not, shall, with your infirmities go quick to hell! But I mean hereby, not only those which are properly termed bodily infirmities, but all those inward or outward imperfections which are not of a moral nature. (Sermon 40, section I.7, Ibid.)

The last thing Christian perfection is not is *freedom from temptation*. "Such freedom from temptation belongeth not to this life." Wesley had a marvelous way of challenging complacency and shattering self-righteous images. In the matter of temptation, he said of those who were satisfied with a form of godliness they were practicing: "There are also many whom the wise enemy of souls seeing to be fast asleep in the dead form of godliness, will not tempt to gross sin, lest they should awake before they drop into everlasting burnings" (Sermon 40, section I.8, Ibid.).

As he dealt with such self-righteous people harshly, he dealt with others tenderly:

> I know there are also children of God who, being now justified freely, having found redemption in the blood of Christ, for the present feel no temptation. God hath said to their enemies, "Touch not Mine anointed, and do My children no harm." And for this season, it may be weeks or months, He causes them to ride on high places, He beareth them on eagles' wings, above all the fiery darts of the wicked one. But this state will not last always; as we may learn from that single consideration, that the Son of God Himself, in the days of His flesh, was tempted even to the end of His life. (Sermon 40, section I.8, Ibid.)

Let me reiterate. Christian perfection is not freedom or exemption from ignorance, mistakes, infirmities, or temptation.

PERFECTION IS . . .

Now the second consideration: what Christian perfection is.

This requires looking at the whole picture of salvation as Wesley perceived it in scripture and experience.

Wesley placed a strong emphasis on regeneration, or the new birth, as distinguished from justification. Many Christian thinkers do not make this distinction, but Wesley had a clear picture of what he called the "way of salvation," in which he stated the difference.

He used the text from John 3:7, "You must be born again" (NIV), for his sermon on "The New Birth." He began that sermon saying,

> If any doctrines within the whole compass of Christianity may be properly termed "fundamental" they are doubtless these two—the doctrine of justification, and that of the new birth: the former relating to that great work which God does for us, in forgiving our sins; the latter, to the great work which God does *in us,* in renewing our fallen nature. ("The New Birth," Sermon 45, http://new.gbgm-umc.org/umhistory/wesley/sermons/45/)

Though distinctive, the doctrines of justification and new birth belong together. God acts for us to forgive us *and* begins the restoration of the divine image within us at the same time. This is the reason the new birth is such a powerful image. As our physical birth is the momentous beginning of our physical life on earth, our new life in Christ is the beginning of a life of our souls for spiritual growth. We are by God's grace redeemed from sin, justified in relation to him. We are also born of the Spirit.

Wesley defined the nature of the new birth in this fashion:

> It is that great change which God works in the soul when He brings it into life; when He raises it from the death of sin to the life of righteousness. It is the change wrought in the whole soul by the almighty Spirit of God when it is "created anew in Christ Jesus"; when it is "renewed after the image of God in righteousness and true holiness"; when the love of the world is changed into the love of God; pride into humility; passion into meekness; hatred, envy, malice, into a sincere, tender, disinterested love for all mankind. (Sermon 45, section II.5, Ibid.)

In a word, it is that change whereby the earthly, sensual, devilish mind is turned into the "mind which was in Christ Jesus." This is the nature of the new birth: "so is everyone that is born of the Spirit." So Collins may rightfully call the new birth "initial sanctification."

Now, stay with me, I'm not being picky; this is crucial. There is a distinction between God's action *for* the sinner (pardon and justification) and God's action *in* the pardoned sinner's heart (restoration of the broken image and of the human power to avoid and resist intentional sin). Albert Outler puts it this way: "We have no part in our justification before God, save the passive act of accepting and trusting the merits of Christ. But we have a crucial part to play in the further business of 'growing up into Christ, into the stature of the perfect man'" (*Theology in the Wesleyan Spirit;* p. 58).

It is easy to get confused because the point is subtle. We must remember that we seek sanctification by grace, just as we seek justification by grace. Grace opens the door, and by grace we walk through it. God does not say, "I saved you, now live up to it." God saves us and then empowers us to live up to the fullness of salvation. Just as justification is a sheer gift of grace, so is the new birth and sanctification.

This is important to grasp, because here again I believe we witness the genius of John Wesley in bringing harmony to an understanding of the gospel. Let me illustrate, hopefully without being judgmental. Albert Outler reminds us that in a strict fundamentalist theology there is a preoccupation with the work of Christ for our salvation, and an unhealthy indifference to human responsibility in the struggle for God's justice in human society.

On the other hand, the stereotypical liberal has a well-defined social agenda, and is ardently committed to the kingdom issues of peace and justice. But unfortunately, there is little emphasis in the so-called liberal camp on the foundation on which the kingdom is established, that is, God's personal salvation in Jesus Christ. So Outler concludes:

> The liberal speaks easily of Christ as revealer and exemplar but tends to stammer when pressed back toward any evangelical notions of mediatorial sacrifice. This is why neither fundamentalists nor liberals have a more than tenuous hold on the *full* Christian tradition, as we have seen Wesley trying to put it together and hold it together. Methodists, in his train, have a less than impressive record in doing this as well as he did. (*Theology in the Wesleyan Spirit;* p. 58)

Is it clear? Wesley put equal emphasis on justification *and* regeneration, or the new birth. Both are works of the grace of God in our lives. In justification, we are pardoned and reconciled to God. In regeneration, the restoration of the image of God is begun. And that brings us to sanctification.

Sanctification is not to be confused with justification or the new birth, though the new birth may be seen as "initial sanctification." Justification and the new birth may be the miracle of a moment, but entire sanctification is the task of a lifetime. The dynamic process of sanctification is to work out in fact what is already true in principle. In *position,* in our relationship to God in Jesus Christ, we are new persons; that is justification and the new birth. Now our *condition,* the actual life that we live, must be brought into harmony with our new position. That is the process of sanctification.

Justification, the new birth, is the starting point of sanctification. "It is the gate to it, the entrance to it," Wesley said.

> When we are born again, then our sanctification, our inward and outward holiness, begins; and thence forward we are, gradually to "grow up in Him who is our Head." This expression of the Apostle admirably illustrates the difference between one and the other, and further points

> out the exact analogy there is between natural and spiritual things. A child is born of a woman in a moment, or at least in a very short time: afterward he gradually and slowly grows, til he attains the stature of a man. In like manner, a child is born of God in a short time, if not in a moment. But it is by slow degrees that he afterward grows up to the measure to the full stature of Christ. (Sermon 45, section IV.3: http://new.gbgm-umc.org/umhistory/wesley/sermons/45/)

So what is sanctification? It is, in Paul's words, growing up into human maturity, "to the measure of the full stature of Christ" (Ephesians 4:13). It is, again in Paul's words, "until Christ is formed in you" (Galatians 4:19). It is a total response to Jesus' call. "Take my yoke upon you, and learn of me" (Matthew 11:29 KJV). It is Jesus' promise to abide in us if we will abide in him.

There are two phrases that I believe will help us most in understanding Christian perfection: *singleness of intention* and *perfection in love*. I heard of a young man who received a letter from his ex-fiancée, which read as follows: "Dear John: Words cannot express the deep regret I feel at having broken our engagement. Will you take me back? Your absence leaves me empty and no one else will ever fill the void. Please forgive me and let us start again. I love you. I love you. I love you. Your adoring Sally. PS: Congratulations on winning the Irish Sweepstakes."

I'd say her motives, intentions, and love were less than pure! The heart of Christian perfection is the will. Kierkegaard reminded us that "purity of heart is to will one thing."

But how can our intention be called *single* and our love called *perfect* while at the same time we know that we are obviously flawed? Steve Harper has provided a very clear illustration from parenting that provides us with a clue.

> When each of my own children were small, they had the bright idea to bring mommy some flowers. Never mind that they plucked the flowers from the bed mommy had worked hard to cultivate. Never mind that they might have even taken flowers from their neighbor's bed! Their one desire was to please mommy and to show their love for her. So, in they came with flowers, weeds, and dirt. With faces aglow, they exclaimed, "Mommy, we love you!"
>
> What did mommy do? Did she throw the flowers away because they had clumps of weeds and grass clinging to them? Did she refuse to accept them because they were pulled from her bed and the bed of a neighbor? Of course not! She saw the deed through the eyes of love,

took her nicest vase, and proudly displayed the flowers on the table. She accepted the act of love, even though she might follow it (at an appropriate time) with a lesson in flower-picking.

So it is with God. He accepts our intentions. He sees our motives. It has to be this way, for in the light of his impeccable holiness even our best actions fall short. The Bible puts it this way: even our best actions look like filthy rags in comparison to God. We cannot hope to match him in actions, but we can be one with him in motive. Our controlling desire can be to do his will on earth as it is in heaven. God knows whether or not that is our intention, and when it is, he calls it "perfect" even though it comes packaged with some weeds and dirt. (*John Wesley's Message for Today*; pp. 95-96)

SANCTIFYING GRACE AT WORK

Now move to the final question. What does sanctifying grace do for us?

First, it gives us power over sin. Wesley was rooted in scripture here, especially in Paul. "Consider yourselves dead to sin and alive to God in Christ Jesus," Paul said in Romans 6:11. No longer are we to be "enslaved to sin," he contended in that same chapter to the Romans. Now, settle this truth clearly in your mind. In any given situation, God's grace is more powerful than the lure of temptation. *Sanctifying grace gives us power over sin*.

Second, sanctifying grace *equips us for ministry*. To be holy is to be "set apart." One of the meanings of sanctification is to be consecrated for the services of God. In Leviticus, God says, "For I am the LORD your God; sanctify yourselves therefore, and be holy, for I am holy" (Leviticus 11:44).

The call to sanctification is a personal call to holiness, but it is also a social imperative. We will consider this more in the chapter on "Holiness of Heart and Life." I like the way someone introduced Mother Teresa: "She gave her life first to Christ, and then through Christ to her neighbor. That was the end of her biography, and the beginning of her life." Sanctifying grace equips us for ministry.

Finally, sanctifying grace provides us an *experience in which we can grow*. Sanctification is not static. When we talk about sanctification, we're not talking about "sinless perfection." Wesley himself did not use that phrase. Christians do not commit *willful* sins. If they do, they lose God's favor—we call that backsliding. The impulse and power of sin are not destroyed in justification or regeneration. They are suspended. Sin is *present*, but it does not *prevail* in our lives. So Charles Wesley would sing his prayer: "Take away our bent to sinning." This bent to sin, the possibility that is lurking there, must be dealt with by daily repentance, daily spiritual disciplines, daily renewals of faith, and daily exercises of love until we have singleness of motive and are perfected in love. So we too sing:

> Finish, then, thy new creation;
> Pure and spotless let us be.
> Let us see thy great salvation
> Perfectly restored in thee:
> Changed from glory into glory,
> Till in heaven we take our place,
> Till we cast our crowns before thee,
> Lost in wonder, love, and praise.
> (Charles Wesley, "Love Divine, All Loves Excelling," 1747; *The Methodist Hymnal*, 1964, #283)

So that's the work of sanctifying grace. It gives us power over sin; it equips us for ministry; it gives us an experience in which we can grow.

I referred earlier to the "trilogy" of grace: prevenient, justifying, and sanctifying. Actually, in our Wesleyan way there is a fourth dynamic: *glorifying* grace. It is expressed in the above hymn, "Changed from glory into glory, till in heaven we take our place."

Heaven was an ever-present theme in sermons and hymns of the Wesley brothers. While he fully accepted the doctrine of hell, and vigorously preached of judgment and the reality of eternal separation from the presence of God, John emphasized the grace and love of God. His eyes were more often turned to heaven as he contemplated the glorious "finish" of creation and the consummation of Christ in *new creation*.

> God will give an unmixed state of holiness and happiness, far superior to that which Adam enjoyed in Paradise.... "God shall wipe away all tears from their eyes; and there shall be no more death, neither sorrow, nor crying, neither shall there be any more pain: For the former things are done away!" As there will be no more death and no more pain or sickness preparatory thereto; as there will be no more grieving for, or parting with, friends; so there will be no more sorrow or crying. Nay, but there will be a greater deliverance than all this; for there will be no more sin. And, to crown all, there will be a deep, an intimate, an uninterrupted union with God; a constant communion with the Father and

> his Son Jesus Christ, through the Spirit; a continual enjoyment of the Three-One God, and of all the creatures in him! ("The New Creation," Sermon 64, section I.8: http://new.gbgm-umc.org/umhistory/wesley/sermons/64/)

With that conviction, it is no wonder that Wesley's last words were, "The best of all is, God is with us!" He was confident of his own glorification. So, while death is a disconnect between physical life and what lies beyond, it is not a disconnect between our ongoing relationship with our heavenly Father. This life and the next are connected, and how we live now and our relationship to Christ is the ongoing dynamic beyond death. Sanctification, then, is prelude to glorification.

There is a marvelous story out of the life of George Mathieson, one of the renowned preachers of Scotland in another generation, that gives us a "feel" for what sanctification leading to glorification means. When he came to one of the great Presbyterian churches in Edinburgh, there was a woman in the congregation who lived in filthy conditions in a cellar. After some months of Mathieson's ministry, it came time for Communion in the life of the church. In the Scottish Presbyterian tradition, elders call on members of the congregation to sign them up for communion. When the elder called at this woman's cellar with the card, he found her gone. After much effort, he traced her down, finally locating her in an attic room. She was very poor; there were no luxuries. But the attic was as light and airy and clean as the cellar had been dark and dismal and dirty.

"I see you've changed your house," the elder said to the woman. "Aye," she said, "I have. You canna hear George Mathieson preach and live in a cellar."

That's the picture. Sanctifying grace: "changed from glory into glory" till we know singleness of motive and perfection in love. "Changed from glory into glory till in heaven we take our place." The benediction of Paul is a blessing and a call to Christian perfection.

> May the God of peace himself sanctify you entirely; and may your spirit and soul and body be kept sound and blameless at the coming of our Lord Jesus Christ. The one who calls you is faithful, and he will do this. (1 Thessalonians 5:23-24)

QUESTIONS FOR PERSONAL REFLECTION

1. Can you recall when you first heard the word *sanctification*? When did you begin to think seriously about sanctification as a part of your personal Christian experience?

2. Look back over your life. Locate experiences or relationships involving preaching about perfection and sanctification, or involving persons claiming the experience, that were negative to you—maybe turning you away from even considering the experience for yourself. Make some notes about these experiences and your feelings about them.

3. Wesley insisted that perfection was not freedom from temptation, though there were persons who were delivered from temptation "for a season" (p. 50). Have you experienced periods in your life when you felt free, totally protected, from temptation? What was going on in your life at that time that might give you direction for living your life always? If you have not known such periods, can you think why this is the case? Take time to reflect and to write two or three paragraphs about this.

4. In the questions for chapter 2, you were asked to recall and to reflect on your own experience of justification. Go back and read the notes you made in those reflections. Have you experienced anything that shows the distinction between justification and the new birth? Or have you always thought of these as one and the same? Make some notes about your own experience.

5. Sanctifying grace gives us power over sin (p. 54). To what degree, and in what ways, have you experienced this power in your life?

6. Looking back over your spiritual life, describe any period that you might label a "backslidden state."

7. Sanctifying grace equips us for ministry (p. 54). Have you ever thought of God's sanctifying grace in this way? Do you feel that God has specially equipped you for ministry? In what ways is this idea a growing process for you?

QUESTIONS FOR GROUP SHARING

1. Invite two or three persons to share how they came to know about sanctification and to begin to take it seriously as part of their Christian experience.

2. Wesley insisted that perfection was *not* freedom from ignorance, error, infirmities, or temptation (pp. 48–50). Does this definition help in avoiding some of the "negative" images of perfection and sanctification that group members may have had? Why or why not?

3. Though perfecting grace does not free us from temptation, we can experience deliverance from temptation "for a season." Invite persons to share their experiences related to this Wesleyan insight, and discuss why some of us may never have known such freedom.

4. Albert Outler wrote (p. 47), "In justification we *gain* God's favor; holy-living is the life-process in which we seek to *retain* it [that favor]." In this light, discuss the relation between justification, new birth (regeneration), and sanctification. What connects these movements of grace? What makes them different? Why is it important to see not only the connection but also the difference?

5. Discuss how sin can be *present,* yet not *prevail,* in one's life.

6. Sanctifying grace equips us for ministry. Invite persons to share where they have seen this at work in their own lives. What does this insight suggest about a merely private view of sanctification as inward piety?

CHAPTER 5

ASSURANCE: THE PRIVILEGE OF ALL BELIEVERS

There is therefore now no condemnation for those who are in Christ Jesus. For the law of the Spirit of life in Christ Jesus has set you free from the law of sin and of death. For God has done what the law, weakened by the flesh, could not do: by sending his own Son in the likeness of sinful flesh, and to deal with sin, he condemned sin in the flesh, so that the just requirement of the law might be fulfilled in us, who walk not according to the flesh but according to the Spirit. For those who live according to the flesh set their minds on the things of the flesh, but those who live according to the Spirit set their minds on the things of the Spirit. . . . Anyone who does not have the Spirit of Christ does not belong to him. But if Christ is in you, though the body is dead because of sin, the Spirit is life because of righteousness. If the Spirit of him who raised Jesus from the dead dwells in you, he who raised Christ from the dead will give life to your mortal bodies also through his Spirit that dwells in you. So then, brothers and sisters, we are debtors, not to the flesh, to live according to the flesh—for if you live according to the flesh, you will die; but if by the Spirit you put to death the deeds of the body, you will live. For all who are led by the Spirit of God are children of God. For you did not receive a spirit of slavery to fall back into fear, but you have received a spirit of adoption. When we cry, "Abba! Father!" it is that very Spirit bearing witness with our spirit that we are children of God, and if children, then heirs, heirs of God and joint heirs with Christ—if, in fact, we suffer with him so that we may also be glorified with him. (Romans 8:1-5, 9-17)

One of my favorite writers is Loren Eiseley. He is an anthropologist and naturalist who can blend scientific knowledge and imaginative vision. He records his findings with the perception of a painter, the words of a poet, and the heart of a prophet. Here is one of his powerful personal reflections.

> The sound that awoke me was the outraged cries of the nestlings' parents, who flew helplessly in circles about the clearing. [A raven had raided their home to eat the babies.] The sleek black monster was indifferent to them. He gulped, whetted his beak on the dead branch a moment and sat still. Up to that point, the little tragedy had followed the usual pattern. But suddenly, out of all that area of woodland, a soft sound of complaint began to rise. Into the glade fluttered small birds of half a dozen varieties drawn by the anguished outcries of the tiny parents.
>
> No one dared to attack the raven. But they cried there in some instinctive common misery... The glade filled with their soft rustling and their cries. They fluttered as though to point their wings at the murderer. There was a dim intangible ethic he had violated, that they knew. He was a bird of death.
>
> And he, the murderer... sat on there... formidable, unmoving, unperturbed, untouchable.
>
> The sighing died. It was then I saw the judgment. It was the judgment of life against death. I will never see it again so forcefully presented. I will never hear it again in notes so tragically prolonged. For in the midst of protest, they forgot the violence. There, in that clearing, the crystal note of a song sparrow lifted hesitantly in the hush. And finally... another... Till suddenly they took heart and sang from many throats joyously together as birds are known to sing. They sang because life is sweet and sunlight beautiful. They sang under the brooding shadow of the raven. In simple truth, they had forgotten the raven, for they were the singers of life, and not of death. (*The Immense Journey*, pp. 174–75)

Now, that's a lesson from nature about two Christian realities that were distinctively emphasized by John Wesley: *assurance*, which is the privilege of all believers, set in the grim reality of *sin*.

Loren Eiseley's story is a bridge between our discussion of sanctification in the last chapter and our theme of assurance in this chapter. The birds "sang under the brooding shadow of the raven. In simple truth, they had forgotten the raven, for they were the singers of life and not of death." It is a revealing image of the style of a Christian. How beautifully and with what power did Paul express it in Romans 8. Focus again on his claims.

Verse 2: "For the law of the Spirit of life in Christ Jesus has set you free from the law of sin and of death."

Verse 5: "For those who live according to the flesh set their minds on the things of the flesh, but those who live according to the Spirit set their minds on the things of the Spirit."

Verses 15-16: "For you did not receive a spirit of slavery to fall back into fear, but you have received a spirit of adoption. When we cry, 'Abba! Father!' it is that very spirit bearing witness with our spirit that we are children of God."

Now, to be true to our situation, we have to admit one fallacy in the image. The birds may have forgotten the raven as they sang; the Christian sings but does not forget the raven. *The presence of sin and evil* is *always an ominous awareness for the Christian. Sin abounds—but we sing—because grace does much more abound!*

So we must consider sin in the life of the believer, and then move on to talk about the song-inspiring gospel of assurance that is a central belief of Christians in the Wesleyan tradition.

POWER OVER SIN

First, sin in the life of the believer. Does even the possibility of sin sound completely out of sync with the Wesleyan teaching on Christian perfection, reviewed in the last chapter? Well, it does, and that's the reason we must face it head on and talk about it.

We affirmed in the last chapter that one of Wesley's primary claims was that *regenerating and sanctifying grace gives us power over sin.* Recall what we emphasized about that point. Paul said in Romans 6:11: "Consider yourselves dead to sin and alive to God in Christ Jesus." In the scripture quoted above, Paul contended that "the law of the Spirit of life in Christ Jesus has set you free from the law of sin and death."

A saving perspective on these radical claims is gained when we ask the right question. Our usual response to the question as to whether a Christian sins is "Of course!" But the more important question is whether a Christian has to sin. The answer to that is a resounding no!

There is an ongoing discussion/debate about the way in which Wesley viewed the role of sin in the life of the believer. He did insist that sin is "still there." However, though sin is residual, Wesley insisted that justification and the new birth bring the end not only to the *guilt* of sin but also to its *power*. Here he is in line with Romans 6 and Paul's description of our deliverance from the reigning authority of sin. When insisting on the truth that sin "remains" in believers, Wesley denied that it had its former "power." It was the "being" of sin in the heart, the inward bent to self, that remained. The "authority" of sin has been absolutely and completely broken in us. It has been drained of its rights and power over us.

It may be true that subjectively we feel bound to sin, but few need to know and claim that this feeling is a hangover from a former bondage which grace (in time) can remove. So here is the key: in any given situation, God's grace is more powerful than the lure of temptation. That's where we must begin. That's the bedrock truth, and it is the witness of scripture over and over again.

This is one of the strongest tenets in Wesley's theology: regenerative and sanctifying grace keeps us so long as we keep it. In Romans 8, Paul uses the terms *flesh* and *Spirit* to designate the alternatives. In the preceding, seventh chapter of Romans, he gives a classic witness of the conflict that may continue to rage in the life of the Christian: "For I do not do the good I want, but the evil that I do not want is what I do.... Wretched man that I am!"

In Galatians 5:17, Paul puts it this way: "For what the flesh desires is opposed to the Spirit, and what the Spirit desires is opposed to the flesh; for these are opposed to each other, to prevent you from doing what you want."

Paul writes to the believers in Corinth and addresses them as those "sanctified in Christ Jesus" (1 Corinthians 1:2). Yet he says: "I could not speak to you as spiritual people, but rather as people of the flesh, as infants in Christ,... for you are still of the flesh" (1 Corinthians 3:1, 3).

This Corinthian passage gives us a clear clue to understanding the fact that sin persists in the life of the believer. These Corinthians were brothers and sisters in Christ with Paul, yet he saw sin in their lives—envy and strife; but he did not see them as having lost their faith.

Paul saw those persons in Corinth as "babes" in Christ. Now we need not get tied up with how long we may remain "babes" in Christ. To some degree, we may all be always thus designated. But Paul and Wesley would not be cavalier about this. Sin, and our struggle against it, must always be seen as serious business. Wesley made the point clearly by asking the question: "But can Christ be in the same heart where sin is?" He responded: "Undoubtedly, He can; otherwise it never could be saved therefrom." Where the sickness is, there is the Physician,

> Carrying on His work within,
> Striving till He cast out sin.
> ("On Sin in Believers," Sermon XLVI)

"Christ indeed cannot *reign* where sin reigns; neither will He dwell where any sin is *allowed*. But He *is* and *dwells* in the heart of every believer, who is *fighting against* all sin; although it be not yet purified, according to the purification of the sanctuary" (*Fifty-Three Sermons*, p. 665).

So here is the truth in one sentence: "Sin *remains* but no longer *reigns* in the Christian." Get that! Sin remains but no longer reigns in the Christian. We need to note this particular Wesleyan position because it is the foundation for Wesley's conflict with those who believe in eternal security, or what some Christians today label the doctrine of "once saved, always saved."

Listen carefully to this succinct word of Wesley:

> A man may be in God's favour though he feels sin; but not if he *yields* to it. *Having sin* does not forfeit the favor of God; *giving way* to sin does. Though the flesh in you "lusts against the Spirit," you may still be a child of God; but if you "walk after the flesh," you are a child of the devil. Now this doctrine does not encourage one to *obey* sin, but to resist it with all Our might. (*Fifty-Three Sermons;* pp. 671–72)

This is what separates a Methodist understanding from those that believe in eternal security. We believe that it is possible to return to sin in our lives to the point that we forfeit our salvation. This is not easy to do, according to Wesley, but it is possible.

Thus it is not a question of whether God is able to keep us from falling. Of course God is able! It is a matter of whether we are vigilant in responding to God's grace—whether we allow the Holy Spirit to sensitize our consciences, making us aware of the "new sins" that spring up in our lives, and the sinful abuses of innocent human aspirations. Being kept by God depends on whether we will listen to God's voice and not allow that divine love to grow cold within us.

Let us restate the case by coming at it from a different direction. There are two widely held notions about sin in the believer that are different from Wesley's. One thought is that, "Yes, sin continues in the life of the believer, but it is not possible for sin to separate a person eternally from God. One may *backslide*, but still be saved—*if ever saved in the first place*." This "if ever saved in the first place" provides a common escape hatch: "Well, the person was never saved anyway!" How can we make that judgment?

The second thought is that sin is completely *eradicated* from the believer's life. The error in this position is that it treats sin as a "thing." For Wesley, sin was not *substantial*, but *relational*. The question is not one of the *removal* of sin from our lives, but of *reconciliation* with God, which overcomes the estrangement of sin.

For Wesley, the new birth is the coming together again of a person and God. God's justifying grace makes this possible, and sanctifying grace is the continuation of the restorative process until we are so at one in relationship with God that our intentions are single—to do God's will; and our love is perfect—to love as Christ loves.

When we talk about sanctifying grace giving us power over sin—and what seems to be an opposite point, that there may be sin in the life of the believer—we must have a clear understanding of what we mean by sin. Wesley meant by sin "an actual, voluntary transgression of the law;...acknowledged to be such at the time it is transgressed" *(Fifty-Three Sermons*; p. 216). Wesley always left open the possibility of involuntary sin, which he felt did not bring God's condemnation. But to sin willfully in a continuous way certainly jeopardizes our salvation, for it separates us from God.

That case was clear for Wesley. We *may* "fall from grace" and forfeit our justification, but we don't *have* to. Whether we *can* or *can't* fall is not as important a question as whether we *do* or *don't*.

There are two major principles of which we must be aware. First, there is the principle of the abiding potential of evil within our lives—the old way of sin, which remains latent even in regenerate persons.

Second, there is the principle of our absolute dependency on God. Even after we have been converted, we can do no good by ourselves but must rely completely on the Spirit of God which performs the good in us and through us.

This is what we mean when we talk about the *perseverance of the saints*. Our continued dependence on grace is the key, but a warning needs to be sounded. Some may hear "grace" solely in terms of God's readiness to continue to forgive us throughout the duration of our Christian lives. It is important to speak of another dimension of the same grace, the dimension of transforming and enabling. As we yield to grace, we are being transformed into persons of love. In this sense, perseverance goes beyond the need to rely on God to remedy continued sin, and on to God's gracious willingness to make new(er) people of us. We persevere not just because God puts up with us, but because we actually are being made to be like Jesus.

We must give ourselves to moral and spiritual discipline. As Christians, we repent daily, and cast ourselves on God's grace. We grow in that grace and move from the threshold of faith—our justification by God—toward the fullness of grace, our sanctification. And all along that journey, we can be kept from falling from grace, kept from forfeiting our justification by the glorious assurance of our salvation.

Fanny Crosby wrote it, not Charles Wesley, but it's great Wesleyan theology:

> Blessed assurance, Jesus is mine!
> O what a foretaste of glory divine!
> Heir of salvation, purchase of God,
> born of his Spirit, washed in his blood.
> (1873, *The United Methodist Hymnal*, #369)

And the third verse of that hymn states it clearly:

> Perfect submission, all is at rest;
> I in my Savior am happy and blest.

WESLEY AT ALDERSGATE

That leads to the primary focus of this chapter: *assurance*. Wesley's favorite text for this, one of the central themes of his theology, was Romans 8:16: "...that very Spirit *himself* bearing witness with our spirit that we are children of God."

Early in his ministry, Wesley taught that there was no authentic salvation without assurance. By the mid-1740s, he had modified his position, believing no longer that assurance was necessary for salvation, but that it was the "common privilege of all believers." Wesley testified to this change in an interesting letter to Melville Horne:

> When fifty years ago my brother Charles and I, in the simplicity of our hearts, told the good people of England that unless they *knew* their sins were forgiven, they were under the wrath and curse of God, I marvel, Melville, they did not stone us! (Southey, *Life of Wesley*, Vol. II; pp. 180f)

Here we must tell Wesley's story of his conversion at Aldersgate, May 24, 1738. We've waited until now to do so because at Aldersgate Wesley was justified, born of God, and received a *measure of assurance*. Recall the bare outline of Wesley's life.

Wesley was a priest in the Church of England, a very religious person who, from earliest childhood, had been taught the doctrines of the church. His mother, Susanna, was an exceptional person. She had nineteen children, and all of the children who survived were given two hours of religious instruction by their mother each week. What a task, and what a commitment on the part of a mother!

Having been nurtured by his mother and his father, Samuel, who was a priest in the Church of England, John Wesley had a conversion experience in 1725 while a student at Oxford University. We're going to come back to that conversion later because it played a significant role in Wesley's life. There are few examples in history of a more disciplined religious person: rising at four o'clock in the morning to pray and to study; meeting with others who had joined him in what was called the Holy Club; visiting prisons; giving all his money to the poor except that which was absolutely necessary for his own living. He was almost neurotically preoccupied with the right use of his time.

He was a man *desperately* seeking salvation and an assurance of his salvation. He was tirelessly bent upon achieving that, and as a merciless taskmaster, drove himself in all the religious disciplines and services that could be imagined. He even came to America as a missionary to the Indians—serving for a time in Southern Georgia, near Savannah. But all of that was a failure, and it seemed to Wesley that his whole life was doomed to failure. He tells us that during this time in Georgia he was repeatedly under the power and dominion of sin.

On the ship coming to America, Wesley came in contact with some Moravians, and they influenced his life tremendously. A storm battered the ship to the point that even veteran seamen panicked. Everyone was terrified except the Moravians. They were calm and assured. They gathered together, prayed, and sang hymns, apparently oblivious to the storm. Wesley saw in them the peace that he desperately longed for, and he learned that they called inner peace "assurance."

In Georgia, he met a Moravian pastor, August Spangenburg, who made a tremendous impression on him. At their meeting, Spangenburg instantly pressed the question, "Have you the witness of the Spirit within yourself? Does the Spirit of God bear witness with your Spirit that you are a child of God?" Wesley was surprised and did not know what to answer.

Spangenburg then asked, "Do you know Jesus Christ?" After a pause, Wesley responded, "I know that he is the Savior of the world." "True," Spangenburg said, "but do you know that he has saved you?"

Wesley's reply was, "I hope he has died to save me," to which Spangenburg pressed, "Do you know yourself?"

Wesley responded, "I do," but later wrote in his journal, "I fear they were vain words." He knew he didn't have what the Moravians had—assurance, the witness of the Spirit.

He went home from Georgia downcast in mind, despondent in spirit, pierced in his heart with the futility of all his efforts and the emptiness of his soul.

After a short time back in England, he visited his brother Charles, who was sick in bed with pleurisy. Charles confided to him that in the crisis of the illness, when his life was in peril, he had experienced the assurance of God's love and felt that no matter what happened, everything was going to be all right. Charles was able to accept each day as a gift from God and to enjoy it.

John continued to struggle. He had labored as diligently as Charles had. He had worked for that assurance of God's love probably harder than anyone in all of England. And you can imagine that when he saw that Charles had received what he himself had so struggled for, he was profoundly discouraged.

It was in that despondent mood that he went to a prayer meeting on Aldersgate Street in London on May 24, 1738. A layperson read Luther's preface to the Epistle to the Romans, and something new happened in his own life:

> I felt my heart strangely warmed. I felt I did trust in Christ, Christ alone, for my salvation; and an assurance was given me that he had taken away my sins, even mine, and saved me from the law of sin and death.

In this testimony we have both the language of justification—"taken away my sins"—and the language of regeneration—"saved me from the law of sin and death."

A friend, Mark Trotter, has imaginatively suggested that the experience of John and Charles Wesley, coupled with the memory of the Moravians' response to the storm at sea, was the inspiration for the first verse of Charles' hymn, "Jesus, Lover of My Soul."

Jesus, lover of my soul,
let me to thy bosom fly,
while the nearer waters roll,
while the tempest still is high.
Hide me, O my Savior, hide,
till the storm of life is past;
safe into the haven guide;
O receive my soul at last.
(1740, *The United Methodist Hymnal*, #479)

THE GIFT OF ASSURANCE

Aldersgate was the watershed. It transformed Wesley from a slave to a son. He *knew*. That's a key word: He *knew* that, in his words, "Christ had taken away my sins, even mine, and saved me from the law of sin and death."

In Paul's word, he did not receive the spirit of slavery to fall back into fear but the spirit of sonship—the sonship that enables us to cry, "Abba, Father."

Aldersgate was an evangelical conversion that resulted in assurance. In his book *John Wesley: His Life and Theology*, Robert Tuttle has captured the essence of Wesley's witness about this experience. Writing in the first person for Wesley, Tuttle has him say:

> To summarize, Aldersgate was indeed a watershed between law and grace. The experience of faith, love, and power, as well as assurance, is no small thing, but the sum total of my agonizing search for the life of God in the soul of man must be considered. Struggle alone never justified a man; but man is rarely justified without it. Man can never be saved by works; but he can never be saved without them either. I was determined not to substitute one extreme for the other. A measure of faith had left me blind to my own dependence upon self-righteousness. I was not to be saved by works but for works. The Aldersgate experience taught me that faith alone was the source of power. The experience of these last fifty years has proven this to be true without doubt.
>
> Following Aldersgate I then had to pursue God as wholeheartedly by grace through faith as I had previously done by the law. I was a "brand plucked from the burning" and the intensity of my desire to serve God (since 1725) perhaps made Aldersgate inevitable.
>
> "Unless the servants of God halt the way, they will receive the adop-

> tion of sons. They will receive the faith of the children of God, by His revealing His only begotten Son in their hearts." Yet I had to keep moving. Faith is a process. Had I stopped there the experience of Aldersgate would not have lasted through the night.
>
> So, the Aldersgate experience was the difference not between saving faith and condemnation, the almost and the altogether Christian, but between servant and son. (p. 200)

A key understanding is that assurance is a testimony to present salvation, not presumption about the future. Once the Spirit makes that witness to us, the witness of assurance can be continually verified. It can be verified in at least five ways:

One, we can simply remember that the goodness of God once shown to us in Christ is the goodness of God toward us for all time.

Two, we know that we have repented of our sins and can continue to repent daily.

Three, we are aware of change in our lives—and the awareness of assurance grows within us as we see changes continually happening.

Four, assurance is ours if we are aware of a new character being produced in us—if the fruits of the Spirit are growing in our lives.

And five, we know assurance if we find joy in the service of God.

There are few experiences that can provide more power in our lives than to have assurance of our salvation. Think what it could do for any one of us:

Our timidity and uncertainty about witnessing would be dissolved. We would not be intimidated by those "buttonhole witnesses" who come on like gangbusters. We would know that tenderness, patience, and understanding are authentic testimonies, as well as words.

We would not get overwrought with our Christian friends who insist on future security, for we would be assured of our present relationship with Christ.

We would be joyous in our service for God, but not *driven* in our works or mistaken in the notion that our works would save us.

We would be delivered from frantic preoccupation with taking our spiritual temperature minute by minute because we could relax in our trust of the Lord.

And all of that would help every one of us, wouldn't it? It certainly helped Wesley. On Thursday morning, May 25, the day after his conversion, he wrote:

> The moment I awaked, "Jesus Master," was in my heart and in my mouth; and I found all my strength lay in keeping my eyes fixed upon him, and my soul waiting on him continually. Then at St. Paul's in the afternoon, I could taste the good word of God in the anthem which began, "My song shall be always of the loving kindness of the Lord: with my mouth will I ever be showing forth thy truth from one generation to another." Yet the enemy injected a fear, "If thou dost believe, why is there not a more sensible change?" I answered "That I know not. But this I know, I have now peace with God." And I sin not today, and Jesus my master has forbid me to take thought for the morrow.
>
> "But is not any sort of fear," continued the tempter, "a proof that thou dost not believe?" I desired my master to answer for me, and opened his book upon those words of St. Paul, "Without were fightings, within were fears." Then, inferred I, well may fears be within me; but I must go on, and tread them under my feet. (*Works*, Vol. I; p. 104)

That can be our experience, with the assurance given us that we are no longer slaves but children—and that we've not been given the spirit of fear but the spirit of adoption, whereby we cry, "Abba, Father." We can keep singing the hymn that Charles wrote in celebration of his and his brother's conversion:

> Where shall my wondering soul begin?
> How shall I all to heaven aspire?
> A slave redeemed from death and sin,
> a brand plucked from eternal fire,
> how shall I equal triumphs raise,
> and sing my great deliverer's praise?
> (1738, *The United Methodist Hymnal*, #342)

Two challenges now to keep assurance alive:

This day, and every day, rejoice in God's loving kindness and in the salvation that is yours. This day, and every day, repent of every sin and renew your faith commitment to Jesus Christ. And the Holy Spirit will keep your heart and mind in the love of Christ Jesus our Lord.

QUESTIONS FOR PERSONAL REFLECTION

1. Recall some experience in the past few months when God's grace was more powerful in your life than the lure of temptation. Be honest with yourself, and describe the experience here.

2. Now recall an experience at some time in your life when sin prevailed. You sinned and you knew it. Be equally honest in recording this experience.

3. What do these two experiences teach you about the statement: "Regenerative and sanctifying grace keeps us so long as we keep it" (p. 66)?

4. Look again at the experience you recorded in answer to question 2. At the time of that experience, did you *feel* sin? Did you *yield* to it? In light of your responses to these two questions, live for a few minutes with Wesley's statement that we may be in God's favor though we *feel* sin, but not if we *yield* to it (p. 67).

5. Looking back over your spiritual history from the time you became self-consciously Christian, has there ever been a time when you were in danger of forfeiting your salvation by turning again to a life of sin and "falling from grace"? Describe that experience and its outcome here.

6. Reflecting on your own recent experience as a Christian, do you feel that you know what Wesley called "assurance" in your life? Write at least one paragraph on your experience as a Christian and your feelings about assurance.

7. Two challenges are given on p. 74, which summarize how Christian assurance is kept alive. Are these challenges part of your daily experience? What connection would you draw between your answer to this question and your feelings about assurance?

QUESTIONS FOR GROUP SHARING

1. Discuss the following two statements: "Regenerative and sanctifying grace keeps us so long as we keep it" (p. 66). "God's grace is more powerful than the lure of temptation" (p. 66).

2. Wesley said, "Christ indeed cannot *reign* where sin reigns; neither will He dwell where any sin is *allowed*. But He *is* and *dwells* in the heart of every believer, who is *fighting against* all sin; although it be not yet purified, according to the purification of the sanctuary" (p. 67). Read this quote aloud to the group, and then discuss the following statement: "Sin *remains* but no longer *reigns* in the Christian."

3. Ask any who are willing to share their memories and feelings about a time in their lives when they may have forfeited their salvation by "falling from grace."

4. In the light of this personal sharing, discuss the meaning of "falling from grace" and "eternal security." (If no one has an experience to share, discuss the concepts anyway.)

5. In view of John Wesley's teaching, invite persons to share their personal experiences related to the witness or the struggle of assurance. (Keep urging one another to speak not just of intellectual beliefs, but of personal experiences.)

CHAPTER 6

THE CHURCH: THE DWELLING PLACE OF WONDER

I have heard of your faith in the Lord Jesus and your love toward all the saints, and for this reason I do not cease to give thanks for you as I remember you in my prayers. I pray that the God of our Lord Jesus Christ, the Father of glory, may give you a spirit of wisdom and revelation as you come to know him, so that, with the eyes of your heart enlightened, you may know what is the hope to which he has called you, what are the riches of his glorious inheritance among the saints, and what is the immeasurable greatness of his power for us who believe, according to the working of his great power. God put this power to work in Christ when he raised him from the dead and seated him at his right hand in the heavenly places, far above all rule and authority and power and dominion, and above every name that is named, not only in this age but also in the age to come. And he has put all things under his feet and has made him the head over all things for the church, which is his body, the fullness of him who fills all in all. (Ephesians 1:15-23)

Somewhere along the way—I think I got it from one of my heroes, Bishop Gerald Kennedy—I connected a drama critic's definition of the theater with an understanding of the church. "The theater," said the critic, "is the dwelling place of wonder." Isn't that marvelous? "The theater is the dwelling place of wonder." But it's really a better definition of the church than it is of the theater. Think about it.

A DWELLING PLACE OF THE GOSPEL

Consider first that *the church is the dwelling place of wonder of the gospel.* Wesley defined the visible church as a congregation of faithful people, "in which the pure Word of God is preached." For Wesley, "the scriptures are a complete rule of faith and practice; and they are clear in all necessary points" (*Letters*, vol. II; p. 325).

In his pamphlet entitled "The Character of a Methodist," Wesley said:

> As to all opinions which do not strike at the root of Christianity, we think and let think. So that whatsoever they are, whether right or wrong, there are no distinguishing marks of a Methodist. (*The Works of John Wesley*, London: The Epworth Press, 1950 edition; p. 7)

I sometimes wish Wesley had not said that. It is so often quoted out of context and gives some the leeway of thinking that Methodists are unconcerned about doctrine, that we can believe anything we choose to believe, and that translates we can act any way we choose to act and "still be Methodists."

To be sure, one of the distinguishing characteristics of Methodism throughout its history is that it has been catholic (that is, inclusive) in its spirit. The United Methodist Church has been ecumenical and open to other denominations. We will discuss this more fully in chapter 8. This does not mean, however, that we are unconcerned about doctrine and theology. When people make a profession of faith and desire to be baptized in a United Methodist Church, we ask these questions:

> Do you renounce the spiritual forces of wickedness, reject the evil powers of this world, and repent of your sin?
>
> Do you accept the freedom and power God gives you to resist evil, injustice, and oppression in whatever forms they present themselves?
>
> Do you confess Jesus Christ as your Savior, put your whole trust in his grace, and promise to serve him as your Lord, in union with the church which Christ has opened to people of all ages, nations, and races? ("The Baptismal Covenant I," *The United Methodist Hymnal*, #33)

Then, before the actual baptism with the laying on of hands, the pastor invites all present to profess the Christian faith as contained in the Old and New Testaments. This is carried out with another set of questions: Do you believe in God the Father? Do you believe in Jesus Christ?

Do you believe in the Holy Spirit? And the people, including the candidate for baptism, respond in each case with appropriate expressions of classical Christian faith as contained in the Apostles' Creed.

We assume that a positive response to these questions is essential as a Christian affirmation of faith and for membership in the church. The church is the dwelling place of the wonder of the gospel, where the faith once delivered to the saints—the faith that has come to us primarily through scripture—is proclaimed, responded to, and lived out in the world.

For Wesley, Ephesians 4:1-6 was a controlling text for his understanding of the church. Here the unity of believers is emphasized, under the classic affirmation of our unity in "one Lord, one faith, one baptism" (Ephesians 4:5). When Wesley talked about "one faith," he did not mean a single code of doctrine. He confessed his indebtedness to Roman Catholic, Lutheran, Reformed, Puritan, Anglican, and Orthodox traditions. The condition for membership in the Methodist Society was not *belief* but "a desire to flee from the wrath to come"—a desire for salvation.

Even so, Wesley was not ambiguous about the "one faith" of the church. He tenaciously believed that the fundamental doctrines of Christianity were set forth in scripture. These doctrines had been articulated in the major creeds of the first 450 years of church history, and were described in the "Thirty-nine Articles of Religion" of the Anglican Church.

Wesley singles out three things that are essential to a visible church:

> First: Living faith, without which, indeed, there can be no church at all, neither visible or invisible. Secondly: Preaching, and consequently hearing, the pure word of God, else that faith would languish and die. And, thirdly, a due administration of the Sacraments—the ordinary means whereby God increaseth faith. (*Works*, Vol. VIII; p. 31)

So when we say that the church is the dwelling place of the gospel, we mean that here scripture is preeminent as the rule of faith and action, and that the real question of faith is, "How does faith operate in the church?"

This is not a simple dynamic—faith operating in the church. My friend the late Bill Hinson shared the story of a newscaster who was covering the story of the election of Gene Robinson, an active practicing homosexual, as a bishop in the Episcopal Church. The newscaster asked one of the priests who had worked hardest to elect Gene Robinson, "How do you feel about what you are doing? This is the first time in recorded history that a mainline denomination has gone against the clear teaching of Scripture. How do you feel about that?"

The priest responded, "I feel fine—you can't be guided in the twenty-first century by a 2,000-year-old book like the Bible."

Obviously bewildered, the newscaster then asked, "What is your ultimate authority if it is not the Bible?"

The priest responded, "Our authority comes from the Holy Spirit working in community" (*Good News* Magazine, May/June 2004).

That sounds like a good answer, harmonizing with the notion of *how does faith operate in the church.* But let's be clear in our thinking. This doesn't mean that a group of Christians can meet and decide that the Holy Spirit is leading them to be polygamous. The church was born out of the Holy Spirit working through community. It happened at Pentecost. But there was a difference with what happened then and the claim of the priest concerning the election of Bishop Robinson. On the day of Pentecost Peter immediately stood up and announced that what was occurring was the fulfillment of Scripture. What the prophet Joel had declared was becoming a reality. (See Acts 2:14 ff.)

What Peter was saying is that the Holy Spirit leads in the illumination and fulfillment of Scripture in community. The Holy Spirit never contradicts the Word of God. If we feel we are being led to do something that is contrary to the Word of God, we must test the spirit, because it is clearly not the Spirit of God. The Holy Spirit will never contradict Himself.

While our understanding of truth may be evolving and becoming clearer, truth itself is not evolving. The church is the dwelling place of the wonder of the gospel, and so faith operates in the church. The world does not have the wisdom we need, and we do not need to bring our thoughts and actions into harmony with whatever the current worldly wisdom suggests. The grass withers, and the flowers fade, but the Word of God, the gospel, stands forever. The church is the dwelling place of the wonder of the gospel.

A DWELLING PLACE OF CHRISTIAN FELLOWSHIP

The church also is *the dwelling place of the wonder of Christian fellowship.* Wesley had an exceedingly strong doctrine of the church. His commitment to the church was unquestioned. The fact that he remained a priest in the Church of England, that he resisted the idea of the Methodist movement becoming a denomination, and that he urged all the members of Methodist Societies to stay in communion with and receive the sacraments of the Anglican Church—all this and his total life demonstrated his love for and commitment to the established church.

Yet Wesley knew that it took more than hearing the Word and participating in the sacraments for Christian growth and discipleship to occur. A deep fellowship for mutual encouragement, examination, accountability, and service was essential. Wesley talked about one loving heart setting another heart on fire. And that's a powerful image.

The fellowship for hearts setting each other on fire in the early Methodist movement was the class meeting. This was Wesley's effort to restore the depth and transforming power of the fellowship present in the early church. He felt the Church of England did not sufficiently provide for the fellowship of Christian people, which he sensed to have been the unique characteristic of the early church. Speaking of the failure of the fellowship in the church of England, he wrote,

> Look east or west, north or south; name what parish you please: Is this Christian fellowship there? Rather, are not the bulk of parishioners a mere rope of sand? What Christian connection is there between them? What intercourse in spiritual things? What watching over each other's souls? What bearing of one another's burdens?
> (Colin Williams, *John Wesley's Theology Today*; p. 151)

So Wesley established class meetings to provide the fellowship of one loving heart setting another on fire. The class meetings were neither rivals to nor substitutes for the church in its ministry. They complemented the church by offering a more intense and personal encounter of faith and grace within a context of mutual accountability. It was the class meeting that conserved the results of revival preaching, and became the principal avenue of pastoral care during the Wesleyan revival.

In the class meeting five questions were asked:

> 1. What known sins have you committed since our last meeting?
> 2. What temptations have you met with?
> 3. How were you delivered?
> 4. What have you thought, said, or done, of which you doubt whether it be sin or not?
> 5. Have you nothing you desire to keep secret?
> (Albert C. Outler, editor, *John Wesley* [New York: Oxford University Press, 1964]; pp. 180–81)

Now, that's a rather tough agenda, isn't it? Most of us would resist it. But the point is that it worked. It started a fire burning in the hearts of people that set other hearts on fire. In fact, it started a revival fire in England and in the United States. It may well be that the precise agenda is not appropriate for us—though it may be. What is not only appropriate, but absolutely essential, is that the church provides the setting of fellowship where people care for and minister to each other. That's the fellowship in which one loving heart sets another on fire, and the church is to be the dwelling place of the wonder of Christian fellowship.

One of the most contemporary expressions of this dynamic is the "reunion groups" of the Walk to Emmaus. Persons who experience a four-day "walk" (a conference/retreat experience) become a part of a small group that subsequently gathers weekly to share fellowship and hold each other accountable. The meetings open with prayer, a call on the presence and power of the Holy Spirit, and then each person is asked to share

. . . moments when they felt closest to Christ
. . . means through which they have better learned about the Christian life
. . . times when they felt they made a response to God's call to be a disciple
. . . and times when they failed to be a disciple.

Then there is talk about a plan for living as a disciple the following week, a closing prayer of thanksgiving, and a reminder that God is constantly doing wonderful things for us, in us, and through us. The wonder of Christian fellowship is experienced in such disciplined sharing, coming close to how Aristides described the Christians to the Roman Emperor Hadrian:

> They love one another. They never fail to help widows; they save orphans from those who would hurt them. If they have something, they give freely to the man who has nothing; if they see a stranger, they take him home, and are happy, as though he were a real brother. They don't consider themselves brothers in the usual sense, but brothers instead through the spirit, in God. (Jim Wallace, *Called to Conversion*, New York: Harper & Row, 1981)

THE DWELLING PLACE OF CHRIST

The church is the dwelling place of Christ himself. Now that's a bold word, but the church is the bold dream of God. Go back to the scripture with which we began this chapter. When Jesus was raised from the dead, God

> seated him at his right hand in the heavenly places, far above all rule and authority and power and dominion, and above every name that is named, not only in this age but also in the age to come. And he has put all things under his feet and has made him the head over all things for the church, which is his body, the fullness of him who fills all in all. (Ephesians 1:20-23)

In this particular passage, Paul tries to communicate the breadth of Christ's power. It is *resurrection* power—the power of God "accomplished in Christ when he raised him from the dead" (v. 20, RSV). It is *ascension* power—"and seated him at his right hand in the heavenly places" (v. 20). It is *dominion* power "far above all rule and authority and power and dominion, . . . And he has put all things under his feet and has made him the head over all things for the church" (vv. 21-22). In these three phrases Paul pours out his surging soul as he seeks to do the impossible—to capture in words the immeasurable power and glory of God's work in Christ: resurrection, ascension, and dominion.

Ephesians has been called the "Epistle of the Ascension," and that it is, because here we meet the exalted power of Christ. In the modern church, we make too little of the ascension of Christ. How much thought do you yourself give it? Does the ascension explicitly impact your life? The early Christians were post-resurrection, post-ascension Christians. They knew the gospel story: a Jesus who was once a baby in his mother's arms—but not that now; a Jesus who was a carpenter, teacher, companion, and friend—but not that now; one whose healing love mercifully blessed all he touched, all he could see and hear and speak to—but he is not limited by time and space now; a self-giving Suffering Servant who hung on a cross, pouring out his life and love on our behalf—but he is not hanging there now. God raised him from the dead!

But more: This Jesus ascended, and the curtain went up on a new act in the drama. Pentecost has happened. The Spirit of this ascended One was poured out on his followers, and the church was born. The ascended One is "far above all rule and authority and power and dominion." His name is exalted "above every name that is named, not only in this age but also in the age to come." Everything has been put under his feet. He is the head, the authority. He has been given dominion. And the church is his Body—the fullness of him who fills all in all.

Do you stir with excitement as I do when you think of that? The church is the dwelling place of the wonder of Christ. We—the church—we are his Body!

For Wesley, the lordship of Christ was the Christian's greatest joy. To live under Christ's lordship provides the experience that Wesley described as "sitting in heavenly places with Christ." But this was no passive stance, no resting calmly in rapture and ease. Christ's lordship calls for disciplined obedience and attending upon the means of grace which we will discuss in chapter 9. Wesley called the church "a body of people united in the service of God."

What does it mean for us to be the Body of Christ? I can never forget how the late Bishop Kenneth W. Copeland answered this question. To be the Body of Christ is to be his presence in and to the world. To be Christ to the world means that *we must see through the eyes of Christ.* And what does it mean to see through the eyes of Christ? Through Christ's eyes, there is no east or west, no black or white, no slave or free, no male or female. All are one in Christ. Through Christ's eyes, every person is of worth and the church must respond in loving concern for all persons. We must not be selective in our outreach, seeking only those who are like us. In Christ's eyes, every person is a person for whom Christ died.

Not only must we see through Christ's eyes, *we must speak with the voice of Christ.* You remember what Jesus said when, on the Sabbath day, he stood in the Nazareth synagogue and launched his public ministry. He read from Isaiah: "The Spirit of the Lord is upon me, / because he has anointed me / to bring good news to the poor. / He has sent me to proclaim release to the captives / and recovery of sight to the blind, / to let the oppressed go free, / to proclaim the year of the Lord's favor" (Luke 4:18-19). If the church is going to be the Body of Christ, we must have the voice of Christ.

And as the voice of Christ, we must fulfill in our world today this ancient prophecy which Jesus declared was fulfilled in him. We must speak with the voice of Christ to human beings in every situation and every condition. It's not a matter of a social gospel *or* a personal gospel. It's a matter of the good news of Jesus Christ. War and peace, human slavery, inflation and the national deficit, how the government spends the taxes we pay, where and how people live, abortion, sexual brokenness, pornography, marriage and family, justice for minority persons, access to medical care—whatever is of concern to human beings is a concern of the gospel. The gospel has something to say for our human plight, whether that plight involves our politics or our economics. You can't forbid the gospel going into any area of human life. No area is off-limits to Christ.

So the church must speak fearlessly and compassionately the words of God's good news to every person, wherever that person is.

Not only must the church see through the eyes of Christ and speak with the voice of Christ, *the church must heal with the hands of Christ.* The ministry of the church is the ministry of redemption and healing.

I served as pastor of Christ United Methodist Church in Memphis, Tennessee, before becoming the president of Asbury Theological Seminary. During our last weeks before we moved, we received bushels of mail. My wife and I were overwhelmed with the outpouring of love. The letters that meant the most, however, that moved us deeply, were those that witnessed to the transformation that had come through the ministry of the church. Over and over again, persons said in one way or another, "The church has been Christ to me."

One letter expressed it strongly: "I'm a member of your church, but you don't know me very well. I joined about six months ago and I want you to know my story before you leave, and I want you to know the power of this church."

She poured out her story—five pages. Alcoholism, a broken marriage, two children now entering their teens, desperate economic conditions, no will to live—a tragic story. Our TV and radio ministry brought her to the church. She became a part of our singles ministry, our "Christians in Recovery" ministry, and, then, a growth group. All these relationships and experiences combined to make the witness, to communicate the fact that she expressed in just four words: "I found Christ here."

I thanked God that she, too, had gotten the message. The church is the dwelling place of Christ. The church as Christ's Body continues his work of redemption and healing

- among the poor and the elderly;
- in the divisions that continue between races, rich and poor, male and female;
- among those who are economically deprived and politically oppressed;
- among those who have everything except what they need to make what they have worthwhile and meaningful;
- with the emotionally and mentally ravaged, those in the tenacious grip of alcohol and other drugs.

Finally, *the church breathes with Christ's spirit.* You see, we're not only a *human organization;* we're a *spiritual organism.* Our life is the life of Christ, empowered by the Holy Spirit.

Nowhere is this more dramatically confirmed than in the church in China. In 1949, after the communist revolution had been effected, intense persecution of Christians began. Stories are now being told of the torture, imprisonment, and even deaths of untold numbers of people.

> By 1958 the government had closed all visible churches. [Chairman] Mao's wife, Jiang Qing, told foreign visitors, "Christianity in China has been confined to the history section of the museum. It is dead and buried." In the early 1970s a visiting Christian delegation from the United States reported, "There is not a single Christian left in China." (Brother Yun, with Paul Hattaway, *The Heavenly Man: The Remarkable True Story of Chinese Christian Brother Yun*, Mill Hill, London and Grand Rapids, Michigan, Monarch Books, 2002; p. 7)

What has happened in China, without outside knowledge until recent years, is the last century's most vivid witness—the church *breathing with Christ's spirit*. The most conservative estimates put the number of Christians in China at over 60 million, and some reports put the figure at 100 million. It has been the story of the "underground church." The church, at least on the visible surface, was dead. But the Spirit said no.

The Heavenly Man tells a part of that story. It is primarily the autobiography of Brother Yun, one of China's house church leaders, whose story of persecution, torture, and imprisonment is heartrending. Yet the way God used him and his witness is the exciting account of the Holy Spirit's mighty work.

At one period in his life, after having been in a detention center and a labor camp for twenty-four months, he started what he called the "Holy Spirit Oil Station." Brother Yun said, "Until that time our church had experienced God's great power in our midst, and had seen miracles and many people come to the Lord. But this was the first time we ever seriously implemented a training programme to send new workers to the harvest field" (*The Heavenly Man*, p. 220).

Everything had to be done in secret. The training, at first, took place in a cave in order to not be discovered by the government. Students had only two meals a day, which they had to prepare themselves, and often there were no meals. The training lasted two months, during which time they were required to read the entire New Testament and memorize a chapter each day. This was the only resource they had—no Bibles, just what they knew by memory. Most of them could quote the Gospel of Matthew by memory by the end of the first month. The depth of the calling, the degree of commitment and the confidence in the power of the Holy Spirit is seen in this story.

A group that had finished the two-month "Oil Station" training was being commissioned. Anointing hands were laid on them and the leader said, "You have no money and you are going far from home. What is the one thing you are most afraid will happen to you?"

The response came, "We are not afraid of going hungry or of being beaten. We are willing to die for the gospel! We are only afraid of going without God's presence. Please pray he will be with us every day" (Ibid.; p. 227).

Brother Yun said, "These missionaries suffered much for the gospel. They had to get backbreaking jobs so they could eat and preach the gospel. Some fed pigs, some cut firewood, while others carried buckets of manure. Many people who saw the quality of their lives and the power of their witness believed in Jesus" (Ibid.; p. 227).

That is obviously the secret of the almost unbelievable story of the church in China, a story written with blood and tears, and bitter and torturous struggle—a story of a people breathing with Christ's spirit.

And the Holy Spirit breathes the spirit of Christ not only in the preservation and growth of the "underground" church in China, but also

- in the courageous stand of the church against apartheid in South Africa;
- in the luminous life of Christians in Central and South America, in their witness on behalf of the poor;
- in the revival that is sweeping the continent of Africa;
- in our local communities of faith that continue to win people for Christ, that serve others in his name, and that preach the gospel clearly and with conviction.

The Spirit continues to blow through the church that is Christ's Body. And as the Spirit blows, the gates of hell cannot prevail against this church.

Does it make your heart happy? Do you feel the jubilant joy of it? Do you feel the pulsating power of it? We are the church. We belong to the Body of Christ. And as his Body we are the dwelling place of wonder!

QUESTIONS FOR PERSONAL REFLECTION

1. What is your favorite definition of the church?

2. How is your definition of the church confirmed, challenged, or supplemented by the definitions we have looked at:

   "the dwelling place of wonder" (p. 80)

   "a dwelling place of the gospel" (pp. 80–82)

   "a dwelling place of Christian fellowship" (pp. 82–84)

"the dwelling place of Christ" (pp. 84–86)

3. Look at the congregation in which you participate. Write some notes about how your congregation reflects Wesley's three essentials for the visible church (p. 81):

—living faith

—preaching and hearing the Word of God

—due administration of the sacraments

4. Recall your most meaningful experience when the church truly was the *eyes*, the *voice*, or the *hands* of Christ *for* you. Describe that experience here.

5. Recall your most meaningful experience when you were the *eyes*, the *voice*, or the *hands* of Christ *to* another. Did you act alone, or were you part of a group? Make some notes about that experience here.

6. What could you do to make your own congregation more fully the Body of Christ?

QUESTIONS FOR GROUP SHARING

1. Ask each person in the group to share a favorite definition of the church. List these definitions on a chalkboard or on newsprint, or ask someone to write them down.

2. Discuss how these definitions are confirmed, supplemented, challenged, or enhanced by those given in the chapter—the church as the dwelling place of wonder, of the gospel, of fellowship, and of Christ.

3. Discuss the collective experience of your own congregation(s) in terms of:

   a) Wesley's three essentials of the visible church and/or
   b) The definition given of the church in the chapter as the dwelling place of the gospel, of fellowship, and of Christ.

   In what area(s) is your congregation the strongest? In what area(s) are you most in need of growth?

4. Share with each other what you could do—either as a group or as individuals—to strengthen your congregation as the dwelling place of the gospel, of fellowship, and of Christ.

5. Ask the members of the group to share their most meaningful experiences of the church as the *eyes*, the *voice*, and the *hands* of Christ *for* them.

6. Ask the members of the group to share their most meaningful experiences—acting alone or participating in a group—as the *eyes*, the *voice*, or the *hands* of Christ *to* someone else.

7. Share with each other the most important things going on in your lives that help you to be the Body of Christ.

CHAPTER 7

HOLINESS OF HEART AND LIFE

But if you call yourself a Jew and rely on the law and boast of your relation to God and know his will and determine what is best because you are instructed in the law, and if you are sure that you are a guide to the blind, a light to those who are in darkness, a corrector of the foolish, a teacher of children, having in the law the embodiment of knowledge and truth, you, then, that teach others, will you not teach yourself? While you preach against stealing, do you steal? You that forbid adultery, do you commit adultery? You that abhor idols, do you rob temples? You that boast in the law, do you dishonor God by breaking the law? For, as it is written, "The name of God is blasphemed among the Gentiles because of you." . . . For a person is not a Jew who is one outwardly, nor is true circumcision something external and physical. Rather, a person is a Jew who is one inwardly, and real circumcision is a matter of the heart—it is spiritual and not literal. Such a person receives praise not from others but from God.

(Romans 2:17-24, 28-29)

A Stanford University psychologist, the late Dr. Leon Festinger, had a theory he called "cognitive dissonance." As strange as it may sound, it's very simple. It refers to my awareness of the big gap between my ideals and my actions, what I believe and what I do, my goals and my deeds. We all have that problem. Paul felt that his people, the Jews, faced the problem in a special way, though they didn't know it.

Circumcision was the identifying mark for the Jews. Paul challenged his fellow Jews and the meaning of circumcision, calling for a "circumcision of the heart." Paul affirmed the call of the Jews to be "God's own people." It was with the Jews that God had made a covenant to be a "chosen race." To them the law had been given. The Jews were proud of that, and therein was a problem. In their pride, they became the victims of "cognitive dissonance." Now, Paul didn't use that phrase, because he was a student of Gamaliel, not of the psychology department at Stanford University. But he did address this "cognitive dissonance" of the Jews:

> You, then, that teach others, will you not teach yourself? While you preach against stealing, do you steal? You that forbid adultery, do you commit adultery? You that abhor idols, do you rob temples? You that boast in the law, do you dishonor God by breaking the law? (Romans 2:21-23)

Paul accused the Jews of failing to harmonize *identity and action, belief and practice.*

CIRCUMCISION OF THE HEART

The core of this scripture passage from Romans 2 is "circumcision," and that is the image upon which we build this chapter—the call of Paul for a "circumcision of the heart."

The problem was that many Jews had allowed circumcision, that unique mark of identification as a covenant people, to become superficial and meaningless. "Circumcision indeed is of value if you obey the law; but if you break the law, your circumcision has become uncircumcision" (Romans 2:25).

We make the same mistake, assuming that holiness is simply a matter of doing the good and avoiding the bad. Not so. Holiness is a disposition of mind and spirit. Wesley insisted that holiness is always the fruit, never the cause of our salvation.

Paul made the case clearly with his metaphor of circumcision:

> For a person is not a Jew who is one outwardly, nor is true circumcision something external and physical. Rather, a person is a Jew who is one inwardly, and real circumcision is a matter of the heart—it is spiritual and not literal. Such a person receives praise not from others but from God. (Romans 2:28-29)

John Wesley used the verse, "Real circumcision is a matter of the heart, spiritual and not literal," as the text for his sermon "Circumcision of the Heart," preached at Oxford University on January 1, 1733. This is the only sermon Wesley preached before his conversion at Aldersgate in 1738 that he kept in its original form and used throughout his life in teaching Methodists. This consistency underscores a distinctively Wesleyan view of the Christian way: holiness of the heart and life, or personal and social holiness.

As mentioned in chapter 5, in 1725 Wesley had had a conversion to the ideal of holy living. He never abandoned that ideal, though it was cast in a different framework after his Aldersgate conversion.

Between 1725 and his Aldersgate experience in 1738, Wesley consistently misplaced holiness. He was driven by the idea that one must be holy in order to be justified. That was the futile process that drove Wesley to the deep despondency that eventually brought him to Aldersgate. One of the decisive shifts that came in his conversion at Aldersgate was a reversal of the order of salvation—justification preceded holiness, not vice versa.

There is a story, perhaps apocryphal, of Bishop J. Lloyd Decell, calling in a pastor who had been disappointed in his appointment. The bishop said, "My brother, I want you to know that this appointment has been sanctified by long hours of thought and prayer."

The man replied, "Bishop, that's the strangest Methodist theology I ever heard."

The bishop asked, "What do you mean?"

The fellow answered, "According to Methodist theology, a thing has to be justified before it can be sanctified" (Roy H. Short, *History of the Council of Bishops*, Abingdon Press, 1980; pp. 62–63).

The man was right—though his argument has nothing to do with how bishops make appointments, I'm sure. Justification precedes sanctification. Still, according to Wesley, Methodists "maintain with equal zeal and diligence, the doctrine of free, full, present justification, on the one hand, and of entire sanctification both of heart and life, on the other; being as tenacious of inward holiness as any Mystic, and of outward, as any Pharisee" (Sermon, "On God's Vineyard," *Works*, Vol. VII; p. 205).

A part of Wesley's genius was his ability to adapt and combine diverse elements into a synthesis, to bring harmony out of what on the surface was disparate. This is seen clearly in his understanding of the place of "works" in the way of salvation. Though absolutely clear about justification by grace through faith, and that good works have no meritorious power for our salvation, Wesley was equally sure about the fact that works do have a place in our going on to salvation. He argued that following the means of grace, general obedience, and "doing" what God requires constitute, along with faith, that which is required for final salvation. In chapter 9, we will look at "Discipline and Means of Grace," one of which is what I call "acting our way into Christ likeness." *Good works* are essential, not as the cause but as the condition of salvation.

This is an important issue in our Methodist/Wesleyan way. It is the tendency of those in the stream of the Protestant Reformation to define "good works" as including all human moral effort. Once that definition is accepted, then salvation becomes essentially a passive affair, and any striving for God or toward holiness has to be put on a completely different track. So we don't have much discussion about holiness in Protestantism, fearful lest we get into a *works-righteousness* bind. This is a distortion of the Christian way. Paul, the New Testament champion of justification by grace through faith, insisted that obedience was essential, thus the ongoing way of salvation was "faith working through love" (Galatians 8:6).

Howard Snyder clearly describes Wesley's genius of harmonizing faith and works:

> The Bible says salvation is all of grace, not of works. It also says we are able to work out our salvation, that faith without works is dead. Wesley's way out of this paradox was through Galatians 5:6—"faith working by love." This became a favorite passage and theme. True faith shed God's love abroad in the heart, which became the fountainhead of "all inward and outward holiness."
>
> Wesley's genius, under God, lay in developing and maintaining a synthesis in doctrine and practice that kept biblical paradoxes paired and powerful. He held together faith and works, doctrine and experience, the individual and the social, the concerns of time and eternity. (Howard A. Snyder, *The Radical Wesley*; p. 143)

So is the synthesis of personal and social holiness, holiness of heart and life, that is the theme of this chapter.

THE LOVE OF GOD AND NEIGHBOR

It is important to keep a perspective on at least a skeletal outline of Wesley's thought, especially about our need of salvation. Again, Snyder states it clearly:

> Wesley's starting point was not the decrees of God nor the logic required to solve theological paradoxes. Rather it was what Scripture affirms: God is sovereign; beside him there is no other god; all salvation depends on his initiative and working. But humans, even though sinful, still have a measure of freedom. And if they turn to God, they can be his co-workers in the concerns of the Kingdom.
>
> John Wesley stressed the image of God as well as the Word of God. Human creation in the divine image was fundamental for Wesley because it meant a deep, ineffaceable similarity between the human spirit and the Spirit of God which even the tragic effects of the Fall could not destroy. Salvation was still possible. But only by God's grace, because sin put men and women under such bondage that they could never freely turn to God.
>
> Like Gregory of Nyssa and other early teachers of the Eastern Church, Wesley saw the will as essential to the image of God. God had given men and women a will, either to serve him or to rebel. Now, because of sin, the will was under bondage. People chose to do evil rather than good. Salvation therefore meant restoring the image of God and freeing the will to do God's will. By grace, men and women could will to serve God. Thus, the highest perfection in Christian experience is to serve God with the whole mind, heart and will. In a passage typical of many others, Wesley says that true Christianity is "the love of God in our neighbour; the image of God stamped on the heart; the life of God in the soul of man; the mind that was in Christ, enabling us to walk as Christ also walked." (Journal, V, 284, in *The Radical Wesley*; p. 144)

For Wesley, it was a matter of the circumcision of the heart that issued in love of God and love of neighbor—holiness of heart and life. As followers of Christ, we reflect God's character in our thoughts, intentions, and actions. This reformation of character ("circumcision of the heart") is necessary for the witness of work God desires to do through us.

It was captured clearly and succinctly at the formal establishment of Methodism in America at the 1784 Christmas Conference in Baltimore. The question was asked, "What can we rightly expect to be the task of Methodists in America?" The answer came clear and strong: "to reform a continent and spread scriptural holiness across the land." That's personal *and* social holiness.

But what does all this mean? Simply put, it means that we as Christians are to be holy as God is holy, that the church is to be that demonstration plot of holiness set down in an unholy world. Jesus said it means that we are to love God with all our heart, mind, soul, and strength, and our neighbor as ourselves. And Paul said it means that *faith* without *works* is dead, and *the work of faith is love*.

Mother Teresa of Calcutta was a luminous example of one who took God's call to holiness seriously. She said, "Our progress in holiness depends on God and ourselves—on God's grace and on our will to be holy" (quoted by Charles Colson in *Loving God*; p. 123).

And another modern person who took God's holiness seriously was Dag Hammarskjöld, who said, "The road to holiness necessarily passes through the world of action" (*Markings*; p. 122).

Wesley would affirm this commitment: "This is the sum of Christian perfection—loving God, and loving our neighbor—these contain the whole of Christian perfection!" (quoted by Albert Outler, "Wilson Lectures"; p. 16).

Wesley spoke of "inward holiness"—that is, love of God and the assurance of God's love for us. And he spoke of "outward holiness"—that is, love of neighbor and deeds of kindness. He was fond of speaking of persons being "happy and holy." For him the two experiences were not opposites but actually one reality. "Why are not you happy?" Wesley frequently asked. Then he would answer, "Other circumstances may concur, but the main reason is because you are not holy" (*Works*, IX; p. 325).

But never was it personal alone. In his extravagant way of stating things, he made clear the unity of faith and action. "Christianity is essentially a social religion," Wesley declared, "and to turn it into a solitary religion is indeed to destroy it" (*Works*, V; p. 296).

What I'd like us to do now is to simply underscore the two separately—personal and social holiness—and then speak briefly about the church as the holy people who will be the primary witness of holiness of heart and life.

PERSONAL HOLINESS

First, *personal holiness* or *holiness of heart*. This holiness has two main components: cleansing from sin and consecration for righteousness. The New Testament refers to Christians as "saints" and those who are "being sanctified."

Have you ever noticed the dramatic difference between chapter 7 of Paul's Epistle to the Romans and chapter 8? In the last part of chapter 7, Paul anguishes over the civil war that is raging inside him: "I do not do the good I want to do, I do the evil I don't want. . . . it is no longer I that do it, but sin that dwells within me." Paul moans and groans, feeling he is under the captivity of sin. He cries out, "O wretched man that I am, who will deliver me . . . who will rescue me from this body doomed to death?"

That's the last portion of Romans chapter 7. Then comes verse 1 of chapter 8: "There is therefore now no condemnation for those who are in Christ Jesus." What a huge divide: "O Wretched man that I am. . . . There is therefore now no condemnation." How do we bridge the chasm?

Some would say, "Just give your sins to Jesus." That's impossible. We don't give our sins to Jesus. We give our selves to Jesus and he takes our sin. He justifies us, cleanses us, gives us new birth, and fits (sanctifies) us for Kingdom living. So, holiness is not an option for God's people. It may be an Old Testament word—God's word, "Be holy as I am holy." But we can't treat it as though it had no relevance for us. Over and over in the New Testament, we are called to be "new creatures in Christ Jesus." In his last word to Timothy, Paul said, "[God] has saved us and called us to a holy life" (2 Timothy l:9 NIV).

There ought to be about us Christians something that distinguishes us, that sets us apart in our ethical understanding, in our moral life, in how we live together in our family, how we raise our children, how we treat our spouses, what we think about war, how we relate to the poor, in the way we think about and respond to issues such as euthanasia, abortion, gambling, poverty, pornography, and sexual brokenness.

In Ezekiel, God says to Israel, "The nations shall know that I am the LORD . . . when through you I display my holiness before their eyes" (36:23). The world is not paying much attention to the church today, and will not pay attention to the church in the future until those of us who call ourselves "God's own people"—the church—vindicate God's holiness "before their eyes."

In the chapter on sanctification (chapter 4), I quoted from 1 Thessalonians 4:3, 7: "For this is the will of God, your sanctification. . . . For God did not call us to impurity but in holiness." In talking about holiness to the Thessalonians, Paul spoke of their relationship to others: "Do not transgress or wrong your brothers and sisters," he said. That was a negative expression, but the positive, simple admonition is, "Love one another." Here it is in a reporter's story of a nurse in the Veteran's Hospital in Coatsville, Pennsylvania.

> It was lunch-time in the psychiatric ward of the Veteran's Administration Hospital here. Patients privileged to leave the wards

had gone to the main dining room. For the sixty or so left in the wards of Building Four, there was a small dining room with food delivered from the central kitchen. Building Four had one nurse and two orderlies to get the seriously mentally ill patients through their meals. Six hands were simply not enough.

A toilet had overflowed, but the nurse could not find anyone to clean it up. She tried to do it herself while she kept an eye on five patients in wheelchairs, along with a dozen others milling in a hallway, each trying to get her attention. Three times in twenty minutes she had to rush by a patient curled in a corner before she had a moment to stop and gently urge him to his feet.

"Doesn't this ever depress you?" a visitor asked.

"Not really," she replied with a smile. "If I ever begin to feel depressed, I remember that I may be the only person who cares what happens to these men. And then comes the strength and patience to keep going, to keep loving them."

The question is, do we do our jobs in holiness? But, more than that, do we live our whole lives loving one another? That's the key to personal holiness.

Chuck Colson has written an illuminating and challenging book entitled *Loving God*. It is primarily a book on personal and social holiness. In one chapter, "The Everyday Business of Holiness," he makes the case that holiness is loving and obeying God. He gives a series of personal vignettes that illustrate some telling truths about holiness. Those truths are:

One, holiness is obeying God—*loving one another as God loved us.*
Two, holiness is obeying God—*even when it is against our own interest.*
Three, holiness is obeying God—*sharing God's love, even when it is inconvenient.*
Four, holiness is obeying God—*finding ways to help those in need.*

That's a good witness in our own quest for holiness.

SOCIAL HOLINESS

Now, consider specifically the wider arena—*social* holiness.

Wesley said, "The gospel of Christ knows no religion but social; no holiness but social." The social impact of the Wesleyan Revival, though sometimes exaggerated, is hardly measurable.

Marquis W. Childs and Douglass Cater conclude that "out of the light kindled by Wesley and the evangelical revival came the great drive for reform movements that had a direct and continuing relationship to the life of the past 100 years" (quoted by Lovett Weems in *The Gospel According to Wesley;* p. 38).

Kenneth E. Boulding asserted, "It was not the economists who liberated the slaves or who passed the Factory Acts, but the rash and ignorant Christians" (quoted by S. Paul Shilling, *Methodism and Society in Theological Perspective*, Abingdon Press, 1960; p. 64).

Wesley was at the heart of it. One of the last letters he wrote was to William Wilberforce, blessing him and urging him on in his antislavery fight in England. "Go on," he said, "in the name of God and in the power of his might, till even American slavery (the vilest that ever saw the sun) shall vanish away before it."

Wesley and the Methodist movement addressed several areas of concern: poverty, slavery, prisons, liquor, war, and education. It is not a matter of recent concern that United Methodists have a "social creed" that speaks to these same issues, as well as to others.

Our temptation when we consider social holiness is to address the obvious: issues such as pornography, abortion, and homosexuality. In our zealous reaction to these, we disregard other issues that are equally serious, though perhaps more subtle.

How much of the righteous indignation and energy of "evangelical" Christians (I'm one) has been spent over issues such as "prayer in public schools"? Let me share a personal witness. I spent ten years of my life at The Upper Room in a ministry focused on prayer. I'm committed to prayer. Yet the issue of prayer in public schools is not as simple as many of our politicians—who want the vote of us evangelical Christians—would make it.

I am committed to prayer, but there is a difference between Christian prayer and other forms of prayer. I would have had real reservations about my children, when we lived in Southern California, being led in prayer by the young teacher who had just come back from her latest weekend with a popular Eastern guru from Tibet. Or, by the teacher—deeply religious, but not Christian—who had just finished a crash course in "How to Conduct a Séance," which for him was what prayer was all about.

Do you see the point I'm making? I do not want persons who are not Christian, some who may be explicitly non-Christian, modeling prayer for my children. I want to give other persons the same right also.

Christian prayer is an act of the people of God who are committed to God's sovereignty and holiness and to the saving grace of Jesus Christ. Any other prayer is what the prophets referred to as the "noise of solemn assemblies," and what Jesus referred to as "praying thus to ourselves." The responsibility for teaching Christian prayer belongs not to the public schools but to the family and to the church.

Now return with me to my original point about our tendency to restrict our holy and righteous outrage against the obvious. The United Methodist Church is clear in its position on homosexuality. Within our Social Principles we read that all persons are entitled to have their human and civil rights insured, though we do not condone the practice of homosexuality and consider this practice incompatible with Christian teaching. That being clear, let me make my point without anyone mistaking my position, and the official positions of The United Methodist Church.

The scripture that people use most in the condemnation of homosexuality is the story of Sodom and Gomorrah. The usual reason given for the destruction of these cities was sexual immorality—and certainly that was a big part of it. Yet when the prophet Ezekiel talked about it, he said: "This was the guilt of your sister Sodom: she and her daughters had pride, excess of food, and prosperous ease, but did not aid the poor and needy" (Ezekiel 16:49).

The point is clear: in our passion to scrub America clean we often narrow the scope of Christian concern. And, by our silence on particular issues, we implicitly embrace those things not on our hit-list, or the hit-list of our favorite politician, thus aligning ourselves with the subtle sins of privilege, power, civil religion, and idolatrous nationalism.

Do we hear Ezekiel? Certainly, social holiness has to do with pornography, abortion, and homosexuality—but it also has to do with people becoming calloused in "prosperous ease," taking no thought of aiding the poor and needy.

We're rightly upset as citizens, and especially as Christians, about the present economic situation of our nation—about the staggering deficit that grows daily, about the obscene amount of money we spend on war and the "war machine." Hopefully, we are learning that there are limits to what we once thought was the endless abundance of the American economy. Government deficits must be curbed, lest they continue to fuel inflation, which is morally indefensible and threatens the very fabric of our national life.

But let's keep perspective. If inflation is a moral issue, as we believe it to be, so too is society's concern or its unconcern for the poor, the disadvantaged, and the oppressed. We Christians know from the Old Testament prophets that Almighty God has a fearsome judgment of a people who would "sell the poor a pair of shoes." And we know from Jesus himself that our judgment will be based on how we respond to the "least of these."

Now, we could spend pages asking questions about social holiness.

—What does social holiness have to do with a morally decadent society that no longer questions premarital and extramarital sex; that has trivialized marriage and brought about a cultural situation in which there are almost as many divorces as there are first-time marriages each year?
—What does social holiness have to do with the fact that hungry people are going without food stamps, elderly people are going without medicine, poor children are going without health care because of the cost of the war in Iraq and the tax cuts for the wealthy?
—What does social holiness have to do with a prison system that contributes to making a criminal society, rather than preventing crime and reforming offenders?
—What does social holiness have to do with the torture of political prisoners and laws that violate human rights for so-called purposes of "national security"?
—What does social holiness have to do with the million unborn children who are aborted each year and the 20 million children who go to bed hungry every night in affluent America?
—What does social holiness have to do with housing patterns that have resegregated the public school system?

I can't answer the questions in specific terms. But the questions themselves call us to a commitment to holiness of heart and life. I ask these baffling questions to make one big point: the answers must be preceded by something far more crucial. That's what I want to address now.

IN THE MEANTIME…

What can we rightly expect to be the task of United Methodists in America? To reform a continent and spread scriptural holiness across the land. What is required for such a mission? The circumcision of the heart which will identify us as those people who are cleansed from sin and consecrated to righteousness, who love and seek to obey God, and who are committed to the promise that the kingdom of this world will one day become the kingdom of Christ.

But in the meantime—ah, that's the point! In the meantime, what is to be our task? Wesley answers this way: "Desire not to live but to praise his name; let all your thoughts, words, and works tend to his glory. Let your soul be filled with so entire a love to him, that you love nothing but for his sake. Have a pure intention of heart, a steadfast regard to his glory in all your actions." (*Works*, 3rd edition, Vol. XI; p. 368).

Our first and primary task is to love and to be faithful to Christ. We are called to be the church, to be the kind of community we need to be in order to be faithful to the Christian gospel—to be the church we talked about in the last chapter, *seeing* through the eyes of Christ, *speaking* with the voice of Christ, *healing* with the hands of Christ, and *breathing* with the Spirit of Christ.

Holiness is *communal*. God's people are called to be a holy community. Too often the church is fixated on personal and private piety. As we discussed in chapter 6, the church is the dwelling place of fellowship, responding to the fact that human beings are created for community and long to be a part of a grouping in which they can be loved and valued for their own unique gifts and talents (1 Corinthians 12:4-13).

Our first task, then, is not a political or social one, though it will certainly make an impact politically and socially. We are to *be* the church—to keep criticizing our message, ministry, and life together so that we become who God calls us to be, a people formed by the gospel.

Will Willimon has put the case in a puzzling way: "We best criticize the world by being the church." Then he builds his case:

> Our social concern may appear ineffective to the world. Jesus himself appeared ineffective in the world. His power was the truth rather than worldly violence propping up falsehood.
>
> Our aim is not effectiveness, but a prophetic demonstration that Jesus makes possible a new social order based not upon *what works* or competing self-interest, but upon his Lordship.
>
> This is not a withdrawal from the world. It is a plea to confront the world on our own terms. The imperatives, "Come unto me," and "Do this in remembrance of me," theologically precede, "Go ye unto all the world."
>
> In its very existence, the church serves the world, not by running errands, but by providing a light, that is, providing an imaginative alternative for society. The gospel call is an invitation to be a part of a peo-

> ple who are struggling to create those structures which the world can never achieve through governmental power and balanced self-interest.
>
> By its very existence the church is a paradigm for a society, a demonstration which the world considers impossible.
>
> For instance, Christian charity will always be more radical than social legislation because the world can never serve the poorest and most powerless. The best it can do is to give the less powerful a little more power and call that justice. The world can never give dignity to the very young, the very old, the very retarded, and the very sick. All it can do is dole out a few meager rights and call that compassion. For the poorest of the poor and the sickest of the sick, there must be hope that is not dependent upon public policy but upon the promise that God's love is stronger than death, and that nothing shall separate us from the love of God in Jesus Christ.
>
> Only the church can be the communal source of that radical hope. We must care for the world by forming the church around this truth and no other. (William H. Willimon, "In But Not of the World," *Circuit Rider*, November–December 1982; pp. 8–9)

This does not mean that we do not labor diligently as Christians for justice and peace. It does not mean that we do not take seriously the political process and work for changed systems and structures, for legislation and political leaders who will serve the common good.

But it *does* mean that we will not put our hope in these. We do not place our trust in any political party, or persons, any economic or governmental promise or panacea.

We perfect our lives in holiness. We live together in the church as a people who have already tasted the kingdom. We demonstrate by who we are, what we say, and how we live that there is a kingdom reality that transcends all earthly systems and programs.

In his Sermon on the Mount, Jesus spoke to Christians as individuals and to the Christian community. "You are the light of the world. A city built on a hill cannot be hid." (Matthew 5:14). Can you imagine the difference it would make if the 150 million people in America who call themselves "born again Christians" took this affirmation of Jesus to heart? Can you imagine what an impact any church would have on her community if she saw herself as a "city set on a hill"?

Peter Kreeft, professor at Boston College, has perceptively noted that "the City of the World increasingly oozes its decay." What a description. But what about the Church, "the City set on a hill" (*Ecumenical Jihad*, Ignatius Press)? What are we doing about the septic tanks on the hill that are backing up and are overflowing into the minds of our children and youth and are poisoning our culture?

A while ago, my wife, Jerry, and I had a wonderful three days, driving down the Pacific Coast from San Francisco to Los Angeles, a part of our celebration of our fifty years of marriage. The beauty is breathtaking, especially the rocky coast in the Big Sur. Along the way I saw a highway sign to Concord, California. If we had had the time, I would have gone to Concord. I would have visited First Presbyterian Church there, because I remembered a story I read about that church some years ago.

The church made a bold and daring move by purchasing the porno theater located right next door. The community was thrilled until it became apparent that the theater proprietors still had several months remaining on their lease. That meant that for almost a year, First Presbyterian Church was the landlord, collecting rent on an X-rated adult theater. That did not sit well with the community, but the church did not flinch. It was locked into its vision and was willing to be misunderstood and criticized in order to guarantee that the theater would be closed and the church's own vision implemented. Within two years, the old Galaxy Theater was the Presbyterian Community Center. Where once degrading pornographic images flashed across the big screen, Bible studies and recovery groups now met.

I know we Christians can't buy up all the pornography shops in our cities. But we can support ministries like Binghampton Redevelopment in my city, which continues to buy property in a community desperately needing renewal—drug houses, apartments intolerable for human dwelling—seeking to make that community "a city set on a hill," rather than one that "increasingly oozes decay."

We may not be able to eradicate ethnic prejudice or feed all the hungry children in our community. Pornography may continue to poison television fare. All swords may not be immediately beaten into plowshares, and spears into pruning hooks. The City of the World will continue to ooze its decay. But the "city set on a hill," the church, will not grow weary in confronting the principalities and powers of darkness. We will seek to permeate the world with our holiness of heart and life, and thus hasten the day when the kingdoms of this world will become the kingdom of our Lord and Christ, who will reign forever and ever.

QUESTIONS FOR PERSONAL REFLECTION

1. In your own spiritual pilgrimage, have you been conscious of any tension between experiencing "salvation by grace through faith alone," and the call to "work out your salvation in fear and trembling"? Describe your own experience in this regard.

2. Do you ever recognize a tension between your *will* and the mind of Christ working in you? If so, make some notes about this tension—how it feels and how it expresses itself in your life.

3. Looking back over your Christian journey, which have you paid more attention to—*personal* or *social* holiness? Why do you think this is so?

To which are you paying more attention now? Are you changing in any way in this regard?

4. Recall and describe some occasion or circumstance when you obeyed God though it was against your interest.

5. Have you ever been involved with a group in a struggle over a particular issue in which you fought for social holiness? Name that issue, and describe why you think the goal of holiness is connected to it.

   If you have never been involved in such a struggle, why has this been the case? How would you explain your lack of involvement in the light of the call to "social holiness"?

QUESTIONS FOR GROUP SHARING

1. Invite persons in the group to share any *new* thought or idea that came from the study of this chapter.

2. With what issue or idea did participants have the most difficulty?

3. Ask each person to share *briefly* his or her personal Christian journey with respect to personal and social holiness. Where has the emphasis been? Are things changing in any way?

4. On p. 102 is Chuck Colson's definition of holiness as obeying God: Loving one another as God loves us; obeying even when it is against our own interest; sharing God's love, even when it is inconvenient; and finding ways to help those in need. Ask the group to share experiences of obeying God in any of these categories.

5. On p. 104, we mentioned the issue of homosexuality and saw how the prophet Ezekiel expressed equal concern over some other less "sensational" social sins, for example, extravagant eating habits and failure to aid the poor and needy. In your opinion, what are the crucial social issues in your community that you and your congregation must address? List these, but give special attention to the "nonglaring" issues.

6. What would it mean, and what would have to happen, for your congregation to be a demonstration plot of holiness set down in an unholy world? Name two or more specific steps that would strengthen your congregation's witness in this area.

7. In light of all that you have discussed, invite the group to devise a three- or four-sentence definition of the "circumcision of the heart." Encourage the group to write this down in their study books.

CHAPTER 8

STYLE: SOME DISTINCTIVE MARKS OF A UNITED METHODIST

For freedom Christ has set us free. Stand firm, therefore, and do not submit again to a yoke of slavery. Listen! I, Paul, am telling you that if you let yourself be circumcised, Christ will be of no benefit to you. Once again I testify to every man who lets himself be circumcised that he is obliged to obey the entire law. You who want to be justified by the law have cut yourselves off from Christ; you have fallen away from grace. For through the Spirit, by faith, we eagerly wait for the hope of righteousness. For in Christ Jesus neither circumcision nor uncircumcision counts for anything; the only thing that counts is faith working through love. You were running well; who prevented you from obeying the truth? Such persuasion does not come from the one who calls you. A little yeast leavens the whole batch of dough. (Galatians 5:1-9)

Circumstances sometimes call us to do strange things—things we would not otherwise do. Circumstances also cause us to do things we should have done but never got around to before.

Two out-of-town visitors were walking along a street in New York City late one night. One of the pair, wary of the reputation of city streets at night, kept glancing over his shoulder, nervously eyeing every alley and shadowed doorway. Sure enough, his anticipation was rewarded. As the two rounded the next corner, two muggers appeared out of the darkness and closed in. The nervous fellow knew what was going to happen. He reached for his wallet, pulled out of it a $50 bill, and handed it to his friend: "Joe, here's that $50 I've been owing you for six months."

According to some critics, John Wesley never had an original idea in his life. He just borrowed from others. But the point is, whatever Wesley borrowed, he paid back tenfold and more. Even if it's true that Wesley only borrowed from others, that would hardly solve the riddle of this man and the spiritual dynamic of the Methodist movement. Wesley's genius and originality lay precisely in his borrowing, adapting, and combining diverse elements into a synthesis more dynamic than the sum of its parts.

Wesley also had the genius of putting an expansive, explosive truth in a single, sometimes simple sentence or a pithy phrase. He encapsulated his vision of mission and ministry in the sentence that has been on the lips of Methodists ever since: "The world is my parish." He borrowed from Paul to summarize his theology succinctly: "Faith working through love." He gave a challenging and rather complete principle of stewardship in the crisp triplet: "Gain all you can, save all you can, and give all you can."

Wesley put controversy into perspective and defined what should be the position of every Christian in one terse line: "In essentials, unity; in nonessentials, liberty; in all things, charity." He described his whole approach to differences in belief and church order in the one question: "Is thine heart right, as my heart is with thy heart?... If it be, give me thine hand."

In this chapter, we will look at the *style* of a United Methodist. Style can be as important as content. There is a sense in which "the medium is the message."

Diana Vreeland, the undisputed leader in fashion, wrote her autobiography with the simple but *stylish* title, *DV*. It recorded her lifetime of living with inimitable style. She made a big point about the importance of style by referring to Japan. "God was fair to the Japanese," she said. "He gave them no oil, no coal, no diamonds, no gold, no material resources—nothing! Nothing comes from the island that you can sustain a civilization on. All God gave the Japanese was a sense of style" *(House and Garden*, April 1984; p. 36, excerpts from *DV)*. It was the ultimate compliment to the Japanese from this fashion style setter.

United Methodists have a style that, to a marked degree, defines our uniqueness. As we look at some distinctive ingredients that make up that style, hold in your mind the fact that these marks are to be seen in the context of all the essential things we've been talking about in the preceding chapters.

A CATHOLIC SPIRIT

First, a catholic spirit. This is a celebrated aspect of our style. This spirit is desperately needed in our day, because too many Christians are plagued with *xenophobia.*

You didn't know the church was plagued with xenophobia, did you? It's not a common word in our vocabulary. I thought about it recently when I saw a TV special on all the phobias psychologists and psychiatrists are helping people deal with.

A phobia is an exaggerated and persistent aversion to or dread and fear of something. Common ones that psychologists deal with most frequently are *acrophobia,* the fear of high places; *claustrophobia,* the fear of closed-in places; *demophobia,* the fear of crowds; *autophobia,* the fear of self or being alone; and *mysophobia,* the fear of contamination. And there are numerous others that are the source of great emotional problems. I learned a new one recently—*gamophobia,* the fear of marriage.

But back to xenophobia. Xenophobia is a "hatred or distrust of foreigners or strangers." Practically speaking, it is a fear of that which is different from yourself, the fear and suspicion of differences. It has been the phobia of people from the beginning, and still is. Xenophobia has also plagued the church.

Peter and the Jerusalem apostles feared Paul and his work among the Gentiles. They were suspicious because they did not understand. That spirit within the church has often hindered the ministry of Christ. We fear opinions, positions, attitudes, and beliefs that do not match our own.

Over against xenophobia I want to put those celebrated words of John Wesley: "Is thine heart right, as my heart is with thy heart?... If it be, give me thine hand." Now, those words are actually from 2 Kings 10:15. Wesley used them as the text for one of the noblest sermons he ever preached, his sermon on the "Catholic Spirit." It was one of the few instances in Wesley's preaching when the scriptural setting of the text had nothing to do with the sermon. Unlike most of us preachers, Wesley didn't take a text and depart from it; he stayed with it. Not so in this instance.

When Wesley sent a copy of the sermon to the Reverend Mr. Clark of Hollymount, that gentleman's criticism was, "Your propositions and observations have no more foundation in the text than in the first chapter of Genesis." That criticism was justified. Wesley took the words completely out of their context in 2 Kings 10 and asked, not what they meant there, but what a follower of Christ should find in them. And from that exploration, he gave us a great word to guide us as we think about the catholic spirit.

Now, two points about the catholic spirit that are very important as principles in the Methodist style:

First, one of the real confusions within The United Methodist Church today is a misunderstanding and a misapplication of Wesley's concept of the catholic spirit. We interpret that to mean "doctrinal pluralism," and such pluralism is projected as both acceptable and desirable of what it means to be a Christian within the Methodist tradition. Taken to an extreme, there is a fallacy in this concept. The way it is projected suggests that a United Methodist Christian can believe almost anything about God, Jesus Christ, and the essential doctrines that relate to salvation. But this is a perversion of Wesley's idea of the catholic spirit.

Such an uncritical, undemanding, unexamined emphasis on so-called pluralism was the furthest thing from Wesley's thinking. He was unreserved in his condemnation of what he called "speculative latitudinarianism," which would be his word for the way many interpret pluralism today.

From Wesley we learn:

> A catholic spirit is not speculative latitudinarianism. It is not an indifference to all opinions: this is the spawn of hell, not the offspring of heaven. This unsettledness of thought, this being "driven to and fro and tossed about with every wind of doctrine" is a great curse, not a blessing; an irreconcilable enemy, not a friend, to true Catholicism. A man of a truly catholic spirit has not now his religion to seek. He is fixed as the sun in his judgment concerning the main branches of Christian doctrine. It is true, he is always ready to hear and weigh whatsoever can be offered against his principles; but as this does not show any wavering in his own mind, so neither does it occasion any. He does not halt between two opinions, nor vainly endeavor to blend them into one. Observe this, you who know not what spirit ye are of: who call yourselves men of the catholic spirit, only because you are of a muddy understanding; because your mind is all in a mist; because you have no settled, consistent principles, but are for jumbling all opinions together. Be convinced, that you have quite missed your way; you know not where you are. You think you are got into the very spirit of Christ when, in truth, you are nearer the spirit of Antichrist. Go, first, and learn the first elements of the gospel of Christ, and then shall you learn to be of a truly catholic spirit. (*Fifty-Three Sermons*, "Catholic Spirit"; p. 502)

So, then, the second point: nothing is more needed in the church today, especially in the United States, than a catholic spirit. In his pamphlet entitled "The Character of a Methodist," Wesley said: "As to all opinions which do not strike at the root of Christianity, we think and let think. So that whatsoever they are, whether right or wrong, they are no distinguishing marks of a Methodist." Remember now, Wesley is talking about things that do not strike at the root of Christianity.

—Does our mode of baptisms—*how* we baptize—strike at the root of Christianity?
—Does whether or not we have musical instruments in the church make any difference as far as real Christianity is concerned?
—*How* we serve communion—is that a grave issue as far as the faith is concerned?
—Is any argument about the millennium—whether we are pre-, post-, or a-millennial—essential to the faith?
—Does it help to get all bogged down in trying to figure out when the Lord is going to come again? Is that kind of argument really a positive contribution to the kingdom?
—What about styles of worship, vestments, musical genre? Are any of these the measure of integrity and indigenous relevance?

Most of the things we get all stirred up about, that drive us to anger, and even divide us as Christians—most of that, I think, the Lord cares little about.

Remember what Jesus said to those Pharisees who condemned him for plucking corn on the Sabbath in order that his disciples might eat? "The sabbath was made for man, not man for the sabbath" (Mark 2:27 RSV). This is what Paul was saying in Galatians 5:1: "For freedom Christ has set us free. Stand firm, therefore, and do not submit again to a yoke of slavery." And how gloriously and with what power did he write, "For in Christ Jesus neither circumcision nor uncircumcision is of any avail, but faith working through love" (v. 6, RSV).

This is what Wesley was getting at when he continued to admonish his Methodist flock:

> I beseech you brethren, by the mercies of God, that we be in no wise divided among ourselves. Is thy heart right, as my heart is right with thine? I ask no further question. If it be, give me thy hand. For opinions, or terms, let us not destroy the work of God. Dost thou love and serve

> God? It is enough. I give thee the right hand of fellowship. (*Works of John Wesley*, London: The Epworth Press, 1950 edition; pp. 7–15)

We need that as Methodists/Wesleyans. The world needs it—the catholic spirit lived out in our different denominations.

HEARTFELT RELIGION

Now the second ingredient of a United Methodist style is what we often call "heartfelt religion." In Methodist language, this is the experience of the "warm heart." This has meaning at two points: the individual; and the fellowship, the larger group.

The Methodist movement was born in England and soon began to burn with a fire of love across the land, in large part because of two big problems in the Established Church. One was *spiritual apathy*. Deism had flavored the intellectual and religious climate. God had become a benevolent ruler of the universe, removed from personal experience. In the arrogant rationalism that pervaded the day, everything had to be utterly reasonable.

The second thing that had happened was that the nature of the church as an organization had become *remote*, removed from life, not touching the people where they were. One cleric, for instance, had been made a bishop and given a lifetime stipend but never set foot in the diocese over which he presumably had spiritual and temporal oversight. It was obviously all temporal and nothing spiritual.

Into that setting with those two characteristics—spiritual apathy and a remote church structure—came the Methodist revival with an answer to these two glaring, devastating failures of the church.

For spiritual apathy, there was the experience of the warm heart. People wanted desperately not only to hear the gospel but also to experience it. So Aldersgate became the model: "I felt my heart strangely warmed, I felt I did trust Christ, Christ alone for salvation; and an assurance was given me that he had taken away my sins, even mine, and saved me from the law of sin and death." That experience was repeated over and over.

Furthermore, for people who experienced a church that had become lifelessly formal at best, and coldly remote at worst, the Methodists came with ministries of care and warm concern. The class meetings and bands of the Methodist societies became the settings for these expressions of compassion. People cared for and looked after one another's souls. Loving hearts set other hearts on fire.

> When Wesley spoke of "social holiness" and "social Christianity," he was pointing to New Testament *koinonia*. Christian fellowship meant, not merely corporate worship, but watching over one another in love, advising, exhorting, admonishing and praying with the brothers and sisters. "This, and this alone, is Christian fellowship," he said. And this is what Methodism promoted: "We introduced Christian fellowship where it was utterly destroyed," said Wesley. And the fruits of it have been peace, joy, love, and zeal for every good word and work. (Snyder, *The Radical Wesley*; p. 148)

One question we need to ask is whether this style of the warm heart is pronounced enough in our congregations, and in ourselves. And a second question: are we providing the structures of care where persons can grow in grace and discipleship, where the fruits of the spirit can be cultivated?

These are the questions Paul addressed: "For in Christ Jesus neither circumcision nor uncircumcision counts for anything; the only thing that counts is faith working through love. You were running well; who prevented you from obeying the truth?" (Galatians 5:6-7).

In a lecture at Emory University, Dr. Theodore Runyon introduced what to me was a whole new way of thinking about the "heart strangely warmed" and structures of care as means for our growth in Christ and our life in the world. It is a new way of thinking about a Methodist style. He used three terms to make an important distinction: *orthodoxy*, *orthopraxis*, and *orthopathy*. The first two terms were familiar; not the third. Orthodoxy is right doctrine, right opinion, right belief. But Methodists have never believed that orthodoxy was enough. God demands right action, right practice, right behavior—that is *orthopraxis*.

Wesley recognized that many who can only inadequately formulate their faith nevertheless live transformed lives in constant fellowship with God (*Wesley's Works*, Vol. V; p. 354): "I believe the merciful God regards the lives and tempers of men more than their ideas. I believe he respects the goodness of heart, rather than the clearness of head; and that if the heart of man be filled (by the grace of God, the power of his Spirit) with the humble, gentle, patient love of God and man, God will not cast him into everlasting fire... because his ideas are not clear, or because his conceptions are confused." Wesley concludes, "I admit that 'without holiness no man shall see the Lord.' But I dare not add, 'or without clear ideas.'" This seems to place Wesley solidly on the side of orthopraxis and against dead orthodoxy.

In another sermon, he lists all the arguments given against aid to the poor, including the argument that most of the poor are not Christians but obstinate sinners. Wesley's rejoinder is, "Whether [the poor] will be finally lost or saved, you are expressly commanded to feed the hungry and clothe the naked. If you can, and do not, whatever becomes of them, you shall go away into everlasting fire."

Even with that kind of plea for *orthopraxis*, working faith, he always insisted that as faith without works is dead, works without faith profiteth nothing; that "all morality, all justice, mercy and truth—without faith—is of no value in the sight of God."

Neither orthodoxy nor orthopraxis alone is sufficient. And what Runyon adds is that even together, they are not enough. There must be *orthopathy*. This means right passions, senses, tempers, dispositions; and in the larger sense, *right experience*. This, says Runyon, is the challenge to a theology of conversion—

> To recognize the crying need of humankind to be encountered and transformed by Christian faith in all aspects of their being, including the emotions, feelings, and experiences. Nothing less is a sign of the kingdom and its power in the midst of the present age. And nothing less than this kind of theology and experience ought to undergird our preaching, our Christian education, our evangelism and mission, and our witness and action for peace and justice.

Runyon then gave three hallmarks for such an *orthopathic* theology. First, Wesley's "bookends" of *creation* and *kingdom*, the fundamental conviction that all creation is to be redeemed by Christ. The world and everything in it is to be brought under the Lordship of Christ—not destroyed, but redeemed.

The second hallmark of *orthopathy* is realism about the present order of things. "We are a part of a world that has corrupted God's good creation and become insensitive and deaf to God's will and way." The gospel forces us to see the alienation and estrangement of the present order and to present the gospel necessity of being reborn into a new order.

Thus, the final hallmark of *orthopathic theology* is the familiar word of John 3:7: "You must be born from above."

Runyon's insight helps us think clearly about how we provide the opportunities for the "heart strangely warmed" and the structures of care that will be settings for the transformation of our whole life and total experience. When Wesley insisted that "true Christianity cannot exist without the inward experience and the outward practice of justice, mercy, and truth," he brought orthodoxy, orthopraxis, and orthopathy together and gave us our marching orders.

OUR WORLDWIDE PARISH

There are many marks of United Methodist style. In the next chapter, we will deal with discipline and means of grace, which are a part of our style. For now, let's look at one other distinctive mark.

It is gathered up in Wesley's popular saying, "The world is my parish." That word captures the style of the Methodist movement—a concern for all humankind, a spending of ourselves and our resources that the entire world might be brought to Christ.

Now, we need to know that Wesley came to this position "kicking and screaming." His decision to join Whitefield in preaching in the fields to the poor and to coal miners was a difficult one. He fought against it. Whitefield was having great success in reaching for Christ those to whom the established church paid no attention. He sent for John Wesley, knowing his preaching power and organizing skill. Up to this point, Wesley had only preached in regular church services while in England. Should he accept Whitefield's appeal and help with the open-air meetings in Bristol? Charles insisted that he not do it. But John practiced what he preached. He called on the Christian fellowship for guidance. He submitted the decision to the Fetter Lane Society, and they decided he should go. Wesley's *Journal* for Saturday, March 31, reads:

> In the evening, I reached Bristol, and met Mr. Whitefield there. I could scarce reconcile myself at first to this strange way of preaching in the fields, of which he set me an example on Sunday; having been all my life (until very lately) so tenacious of every point relating to decency and order, that I should have thought the saving of souls almost a sin if it had not been done in a church.

Wesley spoke to a little society on Sunday evening using the Sermon on the Mount—"one pretty remarkable precedent of field-preaching," he observed, "though I suppose there were churches at that time also." The next day, Monday, Wesley reported in his *Journal:*

> At four in the afternoon I submitted to be more vile, and proclaimed in the highways the glad tidings of salvation, speaking from a little eminence in a ground adjoining the city, to about three thousand people. The scripture on which I spoke was this, . . . "The Spirit of the Lord is upon Me, because He hath anointed Me to preach the gospel to the poor."

Snyder sums up what happened:

> Characteristically, Wesley immediately began to organize. He formed a number of societies and bands and on May 9 acquired a piece of property where he built his "New Room" as a central meeting place. When Whitefield returned to America in August, Wesley was left totally in charge of the growing work. He divided his time between Bristol and London, concentrating on open-air preaching, organizing bands and speaking at night to an increasing number of societies.
>
> The Wesleyan Revival had begun. From the beginning it was a movement largely for and among the poor, those whom "gentlemen" and "ladies" looked on simply as part of the machinery of the new industrial system. The Wesleys preached, the crowds responded and Methodism as a mass movement was born. (*The Radical Wesley*, pp. 32–33)

It's difficult to harmonize this dynamic of our beginning with the seeming understanding many congregations have of themselves. It is common to think of the church in a particular location meeting at a particular time, usually 11:00 AM Sunday, with the mentality that people are to come to the church. So we order our life within the church in such a way that people will come to us. We design worship, with "good" music. We seek a dynamic preacher who communicates well, and we try to provide the kind of experiences that will meet the "felt needs" of people, hoping this will attract folks who will "feel good about it" and invite others.

We become *come-to* churches, staking out a site in a community and being as attractive as we can in order to get people to come to us. With that kind of mind-set, it isn't long before our ordained clergy become chaplains to the membership of the congregation, and the energy of the congregation is spent on maintenance rather than ministry and mission.

This misses the mark of the nature of the Methodist Movement. From the beginning, and at the times in our history when we have been at our best, we have been *go-to* people, believing the world is our parish. The question must always be, "Are we willing, and how can we get to the people, rather than waiting for the people to get to the church?" *Going to* is our apostolic calling and task.

At least 36 million Americans live in poverty. *Are we going to them?*

Seventy million persons in the United States are under the age of eighteen. *Are we going to them?*

Nearly one million foreign-born people legally immigrate to this country every year. *Are we going to them?*

At least 30 million people in America speak some language other than English as their primary language. *Are we going to them?*

We have more unsaved and unchurched people in our nation than ever before in our history—172 million. *Are we going to them?*

At the heart, Methodism is a missional and evangelical witness and outreach that sees the world as our parish—and every person in the world, rich and poor, educated and uneducated, without regard to race or station—every person is a person for whom Christ died.

My friend George (Chuck) Hunter has told a thrilling story—one of those lively vignettes of Methodist history that gives us our vision for now and the future.

A great Methodist leader named C. C. McCabe was the leader of new church extension for the Methodist Episcopal Church in about 1881. He was a prodigious planner, strategist, fundraiser, and mobilizer. Under his leadership for sustained years, the Methodist Episcopal Church averaged starting one new congregation a day, and some months averaged two congregations a day.

One particular day, McCabe was traveling to help launch a round of new church plantings in Oregon, Idaho, and Washington, when he picked up a newspaper that had recorded the speech delivered in Chicago by Robert G. Ingersoll, a famous philosopher and agnostic, to the annual convention of a group that imagined itself to be the wave of the future, the Free-thinkers Association of America. In this speech, Ingersoll contended that the churches of the United States of America were in a terminal condition, and in another generation there would be few, if any, of them left, which, on the whole, would be a good thing.

That incensed McCabe. He got off the train at the next town, went to the Western Union office, dictated a telegram, and sent it to Ingersoll at the convention that was still meeting in Chicago. The telegram read, "Dear Bob: In the Methodist Church we are starting more than one new congregation a day, and we propose to make it two. *Signed,* C. C. *McCabe. P.S.:* All hail the power of Jesus' name."

That was the first of many spirited exchanges and debates between them. The word about that telegram got out, and there evolved a folk hymn, part of which went like this:

> The infidels, a motley band,
> In counsel met and said,
> The churches are dying across the land,
> And soon, they'll all be dead.
> When suddenly a message came,
> And caught them with dismay,
> Reading, "All hail the power of Jesus' name,
> We're building two a day."
> Chorus
> We're building two a day, dear Bob,
> We're building two a day.
> All hail the power of Jesus' name,
> We're building two a day.
> (quoted from George G. Hunter III in his address, "The Challenge We Face," *The Advance,* published by The Asbury Theological Seminary, Parthenon Press, Nashville, Tennessee, Vol. 31, No. 4; pp. 9–10)

It *has* happened before. It *can* happen again. It *should* happen. It *will* happen again when we United Methodists recover the warm heart, when we provide structures of love and care, and when we get a passion for ministry and mission, believing "the world is our parish."

QUESTIONS FOR PERSONAL REFLECTION

1. Most of us have been members of more than one congregation. Look back over your experience with different congregations. Which ones have been plagued by xenophobia? What was the primary "group" of persons who were feared or mistrusted?

2. Has the experience of a "catholic spirit" (pp. 115–118) been a significant part of your life and involvement in the church? Why or why not?

3. Where in your life today, and in what aspect of your congregation's life, do you find the experience of the "warm heart" (p. 118) strengthened and sustained?

4. In what way(s) is your congregation acting out the affirmation that "the world is our parish" (pp. 121–122)?

   In what way do you personally participate in the challenge of this claim?

5. Theodore Runyon describes three dimensions of Christian faith and life (pp. 119–121): *orthodoxy* (right belief), *orthopraxis* (right conduct), and *orthopathy* (right desire). Describe something of your own experience of these dimensions.

QUESTIONS FOR GROUP SHARING

1. Discuss whether your congregation is sick with xenophobia. If it is, what group is it that is feared or mistrusted? Why is this so?

2. Wesley said that a "catholic spirit" is not *speculative latitudinarianism* (p. 116). We can translate that to mean that a catholic spirit does not mean "pluralism," or allowing folks to believe whatever they wish to believe. Talk about this in the light of how you perceive and experience modern Methodism.

3. Invite persons to share their experiences of the warm heart in Christian fellowship.

4. What might your group do in your congregation to make it more a fellowship of the warm heart?

5. Have someone read aloud the material from Theodore Runyon on *orthodoxy*, *orthopraxis*, and *orthopathy*. Begin with the third full paragraph on p. 119, and read through to the end of the section on p. 121. Discuss the meaning of this material and the challenge it presents for your congregation. How are you providing or failing to provide settings where people can grow in grace and discipleship, and where the fruits of the Spirit can be cultivated?

6. Discuss what your congregation is doing to confirm that the world is its parish.

CHAPTER 9

DISCIPLINE AND MEANS OF GRACE

I appeal to you therefore, brothers and sisters, by the mercies of God, to present your bodies as a living sacrifice, holy and acceptable to God, which is your spiritual worship. Do not be conformed to this world, but be transformed by the renewing of your minds, so that you may discern what is the will of God—what is good and acceptable and perfect.

(Romans 12:1-2)

As Methodists/Wesleyans, we have an equal and zealous emphasis on personal *and* social holiness. Wesley said, "As tenacious of inward holiness as a mystic, of outward holiness as a Pharisee."

Now, neither the mystic nor the Pharisee was a model championed by Wesley. Yet at times he came near the edge of mysticism, and certainly a good part of his life would reflect the model of a Pharisee who knew the law impeccably and sought diligently to keep it.

To put the two together in this fashion, I believe, is one of those flashes of genius that come out now and then in Wesley's writings. "As tenacious of inward holiness as a mystic, of outward holiness as a Pharisee." That's a picture we can live with and build upon. It is a picture to hold in our minds as we think about the place of discipline in the Christian life, and of the means of grace as channels of growth and power.

In her usual disarmingly honest and challenging way, Mother Teresa painted the picture clearly in her confession: "Pray for me that I not loosen my grip on the hands of Jesus even under the guise of ministering to the poor."

Doesn't that say it? Isn't that our primary calling as Christians? Isn't that the only way we will get on in being the disciples Jesus calls us to be—gripping the hands of Jesus with such firmness that we can't help but follow his lead?

Following him in that fashion requires discipline. Also, Christ and the church provide means of grace that assist us in the process, and that's our focus in this chapter: discipline and means of grace.

DISCIPLINE IS ESSENTIAL

Scripture, especially the New Testament, is replete with calls to a disciplined life. This is the process of sanctification. We may call it spiritual formation. Through spiritual discipline, opening ourselves to the shaping power of the indwelling Christ, we grow into the likeness of Christ. It was one of Wesley's primary concerns and a distinctive emphasis of the early Methodist movement that the mind of Christ grows in us. It is one of the marks of United Methodist style—*deliberately chosen discipline*.

Wesley preached an interesting sermon in 1778 entitled "The Work of God in North America." In it, he sought to describe the various dispensations of divine providence in the American colonies as far back as 1736. In the sermon, Wesley commented on the preaching of George Whitefield, which was one of the major contributing factors to the First Great Awakening in America. On Whitefield's last journey to America, the evangelist lamented that many had drawn back into perdition. Taking note of that, Wesley sought to account for this "falling away." This was his telling statement:

> And what wonder? For it was a true saying, which was common in the ancient church, "The soul and the body make a man; and the spirit and discipline make him a Christian." But those who were more or less affected by Mr. Whitefield's preaching had no discipline at all. They had no shadow of discipline; nothing of the kind. They were formed into no societies. They had no Christian connection with each other, nor were they ever taught to watch over each other's souls. So that if they fell into lukewarmness, or even into sin, he had none to lift him up. He might fall lower and lower, yea into hell, if he would; for who regarded it? (Sermon, "The Works of God in North America," Jackson, *Works;* 7:411)

There are few more insightful quotations of Wesley than this. It clearly shows his feeling about the necessity for discipline in the Christian life.

In his book *The Spirit of the Disciplines*, Dallas Willard reminds us: "The general human failing is to want what is right and important, but at the same time not to commit to the kind of life that will produce the action we know to be right and the condition we want to enjoy. This is the feature of human character that explains why the road to hell is paved with good intentions. We intend what is right, but we avoid the life that would make it reality" (New York: Harper & Row Publishers, 1988; p. 6).

Discipline is essential. To be sure, the power of Christ enters our lives in many different ways:

. . . when we sense God's forgiveness and love
. . . when we discover a life-changing truth
. . . through Holy Spirit-infused worship that makes God's presence real
. . . through preaching that confronts us with judgment, yet offers grace
. . . through reconciliation with another
. . . through an unexplainable experience of the communion of saints

All these ways are valid and make a difference in our lives. Yet it is verifiable that "neither individually nor collectively do any of these ways reliably produce large numbers of people who really are like Christ and his closest followers throughout history" (Willard, p. x).

Wesley put a great emphasis on proclaiming the gospel, as did Whitefield. He never diminished preaching and teaching the Word. But he insisted upon the discipline of gathering with a class or a band. As the Methodist movement became more established, Wesley noted the deterioration of this discipline, and he warned against it:

> Never omit meeting your Class or Band; never absent yourself from any public meeting. These are the very sinews of our Society; and whatever weakens or tends to weaken our regard for these, or our exactness in attending them, strikes at the very root of our community. . . . The private weekly meetings for prayer, examination, and particular exhortation has been the greatest means of keeping and confirming every blessing that was received by the word preached and diffusing it to others. . . . Without this religious connection and intercourse the most ardent attempts, by mere preaching, have proved no lasting use. (Jackson, Works; 11:433)

Now, there are some warnings to be sounded. We must guard against turning our disciplines into an end. To be disciplined is not the goal; the goal is to stay close to Christ, to keep our lives centered in him. We must guard against falling into a salvation-by-works pattern. Grace and faith is still the key. We are not saved by disciplines; we are saved by grace through faith.

THE MEANS OF GRACE

This leads to our next concern: the means of grace. Again, the key is *God uses, we choose.* If we are to mature into wholeness, "measured by nothing less than the full stature of Christ" (Ephesians 4:13); if we are going to "put on all the armor which God provides" (Ephesians 6:11 NEB), then we must avail ourselves of the "means of grace" which Christ and the church provide.

Means of grace is a phrase used by Christians to describe the channels through which God's grace is conveyed to us. By "means of grace," Wesley meant "outward signs, words or actions, ordained by God, and appointed for this end, to be the ordinary *channels* whereby he might convey to man, preventing, justifying, or sanctifying grace."

Wesley never limited God's grace to these means, nor should we. God may use myriad ways of bestowing grace upon us. Yet there are some specific ways that God enables us to grow in grace. In his sermon on "The Means of Grace," Wesley insisted that the means of grace had no power within *themselves*. They were *means*, and using them did not guarantee growth. Use of them was not to be legalistic or mechanical, but as an opening of ourselves to God's activity in our lives. Wesley divided these ordinary means of grace into two categories:

> *Instituted* means of grace, or works of piety; and
> *Prudential* means of grace, or works of mercy.

WORKS OF PIETY

Look briefly first at the five works of piety, the instituted means of grace.

First, *prayer*. Wesley said,

> God commands all who desire to receive any grace to pray. All who desire the grace of God are to wait for it in the way of prayer. This is the express direction of Our Lord. In the Sermon on the Mount Jesus puts it in the simplest terms: "Ask, and it shall be given you; seek, and ye shall find; knock, and it shall be opened unto you: for everyone that asketh receiveth; and he that seeketh findeth; and to him that knocketh, it shall be opened."
> (*Works*, I, 278f: Sermons, I; 255–258)

Second, *scripture*. We've said that Wesley was a "man of one Book." He wanted Methodists to be Bible people. In fact, early Methodists were referred to derisively as "Bible-moths."

Wesley's emphasis upon the primacy of scripture was based on the conviction that through the Bible, God gives, confirms, and increases true wisdom. It is the scripture, which, according to Paul's word to Timothy, is "able to instruct you for salvation through faith in Christ Jesus" (2 Timothy 3:15).

Third, *the Lord's Supper*. Wesley said, "All who desire an increase of the grace of God are to wait for it in partaking of the Lord's Supper. This is the direction of our Lord: 'Do this in remembrance of me'" (Weems, *The Gospel of John Wesley*; p. 26). Paul put it this way: "For as often as you eat this bread and drink the cup, you proclaim the Lord's death until he comes" (1 Corinthians 11:26).

Wesley believed that not only is the Lord's Supper a *confirming* experience; it is also a *converting* one. His mother, Susanna, received the gift of assurance at the Lord's Table.

> The Lord's Supper was ordained by God to be a means of conveying to persons either preventing, justifying, or sanctifying grace, according to their particular needs. The persons for whom it was ordained are all who know and feel that they need the grace of God. No fitness is required by a sense of our state of sinfulness and helplessness. (*Works*, I, pp. 279f; Sermons, I; pp. 251–255)

A fourth instituted means of grace is *fasting*. Now, this is the one most of us know least about from direct experience. "Of all the means of grace," Wesley said, "there is scarcely any concerning which persons have run into greater extremes than that of religious fasting."

> Some have exalted this beyond all scripture and reason while others have utterly disregarded it. The truth lies between them both. It is not

the end but it is a precious means which God has ordained, and which, properly used, will bring God's blessing. It is certain that our Master did not imagine fasting to be a little thing.

Every time of fasting, either public or private, should be a season of exercising all of those holy affections which are implied in a broken and contrite heart. Let it be a season of devout mourning, of godly sorrow for sin. And with fasting should be joined fervent prayer, pouring out our whole souls before God, confessing our sins, humbling ourselves, laying open before him all our wants, guilt, and helplessness. It is a time for enlarging our prayers on behalf of others. (*Works*, V; pp. 345–60)

A final instituted means of grace is the *Christian conference*. This was small-group sharing in which true *koinonia*, Christian fellowship, could take place. We referred to it when we talked about the church as the "dwelling place of the wonder of Christian fellowship." The class meetings and bands of early Methodism were the setting for this.

The importance Wesley placed in this means of grace can be seen in two remarks he made. On occasion, he stated that "preaching like an apostle without joining together those that are awakened and training them up in the ways of God, is only begetting children for the murderer." This was his opinion after a visit of Pembrokeshire where there were no regular societies. His evaluation was that "the consequence is that nine of the ten once-awakened are now faster asleep than ever." He was fully convinced that wherever this dimension of discipleship was lost, Methodism would cease to be a vital movement. (*John Wesley's Message for Today*; p. 84)

These are the works of piety, or the instituted means of grace: prayer, scripture, the Lord's Supper, fasting, and Christian conferencing.

Wesley gave instructions as to how these means should be used.

First, always retain a lively sense, that God is above all means. Have a care, therefore, of limiting the Almighty. He does whatsoever and whensoever it pleaseth Him.

Secondly, before you use any means, let it be deeply impressed on your soul—there is no power in this. It is, in itself, a poor, dead, empty thing: separate from God, it is a dry leaf, a shadow. . . . But, because God bids, therefore I do; . . . I wait for His free mercy, whereof cometh my salvation.

Thirdly, in using all means, seek God alone. In and through every outward thing, look singly to the power of His Spirit, and the merits of His Son. (*Fifty-Three Sermons*, "The Means of Grace"; pp. 183–184)

WORKS OF MERCY

Now a word about the prudential means of grace, or works of mercy. Apart from attending upon all the ordinances of God, Wesley listed two: One, doing no harm; two, doing good. Now, isn't that simple? Yet, how profound in implication—doing no harm, and doing good.

It was clearly underscored in Hebrews: "Pursue peace with everyone, and the holiness without which no one will see the Lord. See to it that no one fails to obtain the grace of God; that no root of bitterness springs up and causes trouble, and through it many become defiled" (Hebrews 12:14-15).

Put simply, the truth is this: *to act as a Christian is a means of grace*. Have you ever thought of it that way? Acting as a Christian expresses itself in what we do, and what we refuse to do. It is true, as the song says, "They will know we are Christians by our love." It is also true that what we refrain from doing may be the needed, telling witness of our lives.

Often when Christians think about what they should *refrain* from doing, sins of the flesh come to mind. Refraining from those goes without saying, so let's look at some other areas:

—Your refusal to order your social life around the cocktail circuit may be a telling witness for the Christian faith.

—Refraining from sharing in, even listening to, destructive gossip, and refusing to affirm the racial bigotry of those around us—either may be an act of grace.

—Refusing to treat any person, whether a mate or an employee, as a thing rather than a person—that's a means of grace. Have you ever stopped to consider the harm we do to other people by not valuing them as persons, or by ignoring, shunning, or not giving them our attention—by failing to be present to them?

—Diligently disciplining ourselves to withstand the pressure of affluence that measures life by what we consume and the toys we enjoy becomes a means of grace for ourselves and a challenging witness to others.

We could go on. In our everyday life of acting as a Christian, what we do and what we refrain from doing are means of grace.

There is also a sense in which we act our way into Christlikeness. I've never seen persons who *studied* their way into Christlikeness. I've never seen persons who *prayed* or *worshiped* their way into Christlikeness. But I've known countless people who have *acted* their way into Christlikeness.

The likeness of Christ shines forth from their lives. All of these people pray; some of them are people with a deep prayer life. They study to varying degrees. They worship. But most of all, they are people whose acts of mercy make them "look like" Jesus.

So what we do or refuse to do in obedience to God becomes a channel of God's grace, which transforms us into the likeness of Christ. And likewise, what we do or refrain from doing in obedience to God becomes a channel for the grace of God to others.

One of the characteristic phrases of Paul in the New Testament is "in Christ." Paul defined a Christian as "a person in Christ." It is interesting that Paul does not tell about his Damascus Road experience in descriptive detail. Luke records that dramatic event in the Acts of the Apostles. Paul himself doesn't recount an outward description of the experience—being struck down by a blinding light, and hearing the voice of Christ. Rather, he talks about the *meaning* of that experience in a one-sentence autobiography: "I have been crucified with Christ; it is no longer I who live, but Christ who lives in me; and the life I now live in the flesh I live by faith in the Son of God, who loved me and gave himself for me" (Galatians 2:20 RSV)

Jacopone da Todi (1230–1306) was an Italian poet and ascetic who defined a saint as "one in whom Christ is felt to live again." That's who we are, *albeit saints in the making*. And the *making* requires acting. We do act our way into Christlikeness.

There is a sign in Latin over the doorway of a dining room in San Francisco that says *Caritate Dei*. This dining room is in St. Anthony's Catholic Church and feeds some 1,000 needy folks each day. I read a story in the newspaper about a fellow, a young mechanic from Chicago, who went to San Francisco for a vacation, got drunk, was rolled, and ended up in jail without a penny. In jail, he learned of St. Anthony's and went there for a meal when he got out, before he headed back to Chicago. A woman began cleaning the adjoining table. "When do we get down on our knees, lady?" the Chicago mechanic called to her.

"You don't here."

The young man winks and pulls his red beard. "Then, when's the sermon, the lecture, huh?"

"Aren't any," she replies.

"What's the gimmick?" he persists. His smile is hesitant; he looks uncomfortable.

The well-dressed woman brushes her hair back. She points to a Latin inscription over the entrance: "*Caritate Dei.*"

The brash young traveler squints up at it and slurs the unfamiliar words. "What's it mean, lady?"

"Out of love for God," she says with a smile and moves to clear another table.

That's one way grace comes to us, and the way it comes to others, in *acts of mercy*; and that grace will eventually prevail. That's the style of a United Methodist—disciplined and using all the means of grace that we might hold on to the hands of Christ and serve others "out of the love of God."

QUESTIONS FOR PERSONAL REFLECTION

1. Wesley described and recommended a number of "instituted means of grace"—prayer, scripture, the Lord's Supper, fasting, and Christian conference (pp. 132–134). Describe something of your own practice of each of these.

   Which of these means of grace is the most meaningful to you at this time in your life, and why?

   In which of them do you most need to grow and to expand your experience?

2. Recall your most meaningful experience of any one of these means of grace. Make some notes about that experience here.

3. Now think for a moment about the "prudential means of grace"—about works of mercy such as avoiding evil and injustice and doing good to others (pp. 135–136). We often think of "good works" more as a *result* than as a *means* of grace. In your own experience, how have works of mercy been a means of grace, both for yourself and for others?

4. Who is the most Christlike person you know? Write two or three paragraphs describing that person.

   Now think about the person you have described. How do you think he or she became so Christlike?

QUESTIONS FOR GROUP SHARING

1. Invite persons to share their experiences of the instituted means of grace: Which of the means do they practice? Which do they find most meaningful?

2. Talk about why some of the means are seldom, maybe never, practiced.

3. Discuss how this study group has been a discipline of Christian conferencing.

4. Invite two or three people to describe the most Christlike person they know. After each description, ask the group to name the things that characterize the person. Are there any traits that all of the persons seem to have in common?

5. Discuss the role of the instituted and the prudential means of grace in the Christlike lives of the persons described in the previous question. Are the means of grace obvious or hidden in their lives?

6. Respond to the author's claim (pp. 135–136) that, in his experience, most people who are Christlike have *acted* their way into Christlikeness.

CHAPTER 10

A RESPONSE TO CALVINISM

"For God so loved the world that he gave his only Son, so that everyone who believes in him may not perish but may have eternal life. Indeed, God did not send the Son into the world to condemn the world, but in order that the world might be saved through him. Those who believe in him are not condemned; but those who do not believe are condemned already, because they have not believed in the name of the only Son of God." (John 3:16-18)

For while we were still weak, at the right Christ died for the ungodly. Indeed, rarely will anyone die for a righteous person—though perhaps for a good person someone might actually dare to die. But God proves his love for us in that while we still were sinners Christ died for us. Much more surely then, now that we have been justified by his blood, will we be saved through him from the wrath of God. For if while we were enemies, we were reconciled to God through the death of his Son, much more surely having been reconciled, will we be saved by his life. (Romans 5:6-10)

We turn now to a response to Calvinism, the branch of evangelical Protestantism that is markedly different in doctrine to the Methodist/Wesleyan way. We do this not to argue or debate but in response to an aggressive effort on the part of Calvinism to make its case by contrasting itself to Arminianism. First, a word about Arminianism, the theological "school" out of which the Methodist/Wesleyan way came.

Arminianism gets its name from a controversial Dutch pastor who championed the notion of divine-human cooperation in salvation, contrasted to the rigid notion that God is the all-determining reality in salvation and free human participation is excluded. Jacob Arminius would be called a synergist. He and his followers, known as "Remonstrants," were aggressive in pointing out that many Protestants before them were synergists in some sense of the word. Though the word may have many positive and negative meanings in theological discussion, here it simply means any belief in human responsibility and the graciously given ability to freely accept or reject the grace of salvation.

Robert E. Olson reminds us that Philip Melanchthon (1497–1560), Martin Luther's lieutenant in the German Reformation, was a synergist, but Luther wasn't. "Because of Melanchthon's influence on post-Luther Lutheranism, many Lutherans throughout Europe adopted a synergistic outlook on salvation, eschewing unconditional predestination and affirming that grace is resistible" (*Arminian Theology*, InterVarsity Press, 2006, p. 14). As Olson puts it,

> Arminian theology was at first suppressed in the United Provinces (known today as the Netherlands) but caught on there later and spread to England and the American colonies, largely through the influence of John Wesley and the Methodists. Many early Baptists (General Baptists) were Arminians, as many are today. Numerous denominations are devoted to Arminian theology, even where the label is not used. These include all Pentecostals, Restorationists (Churches of Christ and other denominations rooted in the revivals of Alexander Campbell), Methodists (and all off-shoots of Methodism, including the large Holiness movement) and many if not all Baptists. The influence of Arminius and Arminian theology is deep and broad in Protestant theology. (Olson; p. 14)

The debate between Arminianism and Calvinism is most often framed by the concept of freedom. The distinction is too often too simply stated: the tension or conflict between God's sovereign right to do what he chooses with his creation (Calvinism) and humanity's ability to shape its own destiny (Arminianism). We will return to this notion. For now, be clear of the broad picture. Both Arminianism and Calvinism affirm divine sovereignty, though they differ profoundly in how God has chosen to express his sovereignty. Both claim and embrace the absolute necessity of grace for anything good in human life. Both believe and contend that salvation is a free gift that can only be received by faith apart from any meritorious human works of righteousness. Both affirm the divine initiative of grace as the first step in salvation, and deny any human ability to initiate a relationship with God by exercising a goodwill toward God.

Expressing the issue in terms of the controversy between Calvinism and Arminianism—both forms of Protestantism—they take different approaches to salvation. Both believe in salvation by grace through faith alone as opposed to salvation by grace through faith and good works. Both deny that any part of salvation can be based on human merit. Both affirm the sole supreme authority of Scripture and the priesthood of all believers. All of these are the core issues of Protestant theology.

The primary distinction is the Arminian denial of Calvinism's belief in unconditional reprobation, God's choice not to save some persons and thereby consign them to an eternity in hell. Because of this denial, it follows that Arminians oppose "unconditional election," the selection of some persons out of the mass of all sinners to be saved apart from anything God sees in them, except that in his sovereignty he has elected them for salvation. The two cannot be separated. If we affirm God's unconditional selection of some to salvation, we must affirm that all others are selected to reprobation. Arminians believe this impugns the very character of God.

That brings us back to the fact that debate between Calvinism and Arminianism is most often framed by the concept of freedom: God's sovereignty and human freedom. Even so, Calvinists tend to view human freedom as a threat to divine sovereignty. The Wesleyan/Arminian claim is that freedom as a gift does not violate God's sovereignty but rather affirms it. Human freedom is God's creation gift at the outset. From the beginning it is something God calls "good" (Genesis 1 and 2), even if it has become tainted and self-centered after the fall. We may put it this way: Calvinists tend to have a strong view of the fall but too weak a view of creation at the outset.

However, when freedom becomes the center of debate, the issue of power becomes prominent. Is the sovereign God of the universe in control, or is sinful humanity at the helm? Does the Almighty Creator God have the right and the power to do what he pleases with his creation? As someone put it, "It is easy to see the attraction of Calvinism when the debate is transformed into a court hearing with Calvinism defending the majesty of God and Arminianism representing the rights of humanity" (Jerry L. Walls and Joseph R. Dongell, *Why I Am Not a Calvinist*, InterVarsity Press, 2004, p. 8).

Sovereignty and power are indeed important issues, but the truly fundamental issue is not God's power but God's character of holy love.

Since this book is about salvation and in the previous nine chapters I have sought to provide a study in the Wesleyan tradition, this chapter is meaningful only if we acknowledge and grapple with the Calvinist (Reformed) account of salvation. That understanding has been spelled out in five claims, summarized in what may be the most famous acronym in the history of theology: TULIP.

Total depravity
Unconditional election
Limited atonement
Irresistible grace
Perseverance of the saints

Total depravity describes the desperate condition of fallen sinners apart from the grace of God. As we made clear in chapter 3, Wesley and we Methodists believe that sin is universal. Not just the proneness to sin, but sin itself, is a part of every human life, affecting every facet of life and the human personality, making us incapable of doing good or loving God as we should. So Arminians/Methodists are in essential agreement with Calvinists and many other Christian traditions on the issue of total depravity. However, differences arise when we ask how God deals with sinners in their desperate condition. Our Methodist/Wesleyan response to the question puts us at odds with Calvinism. Thus our disagreement with the middle three TULIP principles: unconditional election, limited atonement, and irresistible grace.

Calvinism contends that God has chosen to rescue certain specific fallen sinners from their helpless and hopeless condition, leaving the rest of humanity to perish eternally. Atonement is therefore limited only to those persons God has unconditionally chosen to save. We Wesleyans believe that God's atonement through the death of Jesus Christ is for all. (See John 3:16-18; Romans 5:6-8.)

The atonement of Jesus Christ is not limited, as the Calvinists insist. Through his prevenient grace, which we discussed in chapter 2, the Lord seeks us before we begin to seek him. Wesley sounded this note strongly in opposition to the Calvinist position that some are unconditionally elected for salvation and the rest consigned to hell. Grace is universal, "free in all, and free for all." This means that grace is given by God without price, demanding nothing of us before it is bestowed, flowing from the free mercy of God, not limited to those who are unconditionally elected for salvation.

Again, as stated in chapter 2, this doesn't mean that all persons receive this grace, or that they deliberately appropriate it, or respond to it for their salvation. It is not, as Calvinism contends, irresistible grace. Calvinism would have to claim this. If God unconditionally elects who will be saved according to his sovereign will, and if the atonement of Christ is limited to those chosen for salvation, then it follows that the elect are not able to resist God's sovereign choice to save them.

The Methodist/Wesleyan understanding of salvation involves the freedom of persons to respond to the grace freely offered by God in Jesus Christ. This is the synergy in Arminian thought mentioned earlier. Calvinists accuse Arminians of diminishing God's sovereignty in our insistence on the human capacity to respond. Arminians respond that our freedom is God's gift and does not take anything from God's freedom or sovereignty.

Calvinists tend to regard synergism as equal cooperation between God and a human in salvation, arguing that this makes the human contribution crucial and efficacious to salvation. This is not the Arminian synergism. All the power, ability, and efficacy in salvation is grace, and this is God's gift. Yet God allows humans the ability to resist or not resist God's grace. The only contribution humans make is nonresistance to grace.

Arminius offered a rather simple analogy to explain the "concurrence and agreement of divine grace with free will":

> A rich man bestows, on a poor and famishing beggar, alms by which he may be able to maintain himself and his family. Does it cease to be a pure gift, because the beggar extends his hand to receive it? Can it be said with propriety, that "the alms depended partly on the liberality of the Donor, and partly on the liberality of the Receiver," though the latter would not have possessed the alms unless he had received it by stretching out his hand? Can it be correctly said, because the beggar is always prepared to receive, that "he can have the alms, or not have it, just as he pleases?" If these assertions cannot be truly made about a beggar who receives alms, how much less can they be made about the gift of faith, for the receiving of which far more Acts of Divine Grace are required! (Arminius, "The Apology or Defense of James Arminius, D.D.," *Works*, 2:52, quoted by Olson, p. 165)

So while Arminians and Calvinists are in basic agreement on the issue of total depravity, they are in complete disagreement on the middle three principles of TULIP: unconditional election, limited atonement, and irresistible grace.

The fifth TULIP principle is perseverance of the saints. This principle follows logically the belief that election is unconditional, that the atonement is only for those who are elected, and the grace that saves the elect is irresistible. There is no option: God in his sovereignty will sustain the chosen in faith, thus accomplishing the final salvation for which he elected them.

This notion of the perseverance of the saints often goes under the label "eternal security." This doctrine is often affirmed by those who are not Calvinist in the full TULIP sense—for example, many Baptists. It is certainly possible, as is the case with many forms of Baptists, to affirm and defend eternal security while rejecting unconditional salvation, limited atonement, and irresistible grace.

For much the same reasons that we deny unconditional election, limited atonement, and irresistible grace, as Methodists/Wesleyans we do not claim the perseverance of the saints or "eternal security" in the same way Calvinists do. As we indicated in chapter 5, we believe that saints do persevere, but they do so by the grace of God, and they do so by being vigilant in responding to God's grace, continually allowing the Holy Spirit to sensitize our consciences, and remaining absolutely dependent upon God's grace. It is possible, however, for persons who were at one time "saints" to resist God's grace and reject a saving relationship with God.

We discussed this issue in chapter 5, as we considered assurance, which is the privilege of all believers. We will look again at assurance, but here in the matter of "eternal security," there is a fundamental principle to underscore relating to human freedom and the continuing presence of sin in the life of the believer. I like the way Carl Bangs, in his biography, described Arminius's objective as a "theology of grace which does not leave man a 'stock or a stone'" because for him "grace is not a force but a person" (*Arminius*, Zondervan, 1985; pp. 195, 343). Arminius was concerned not only that God not be made the author of sin but that man not be reduced to an automaton as Calvinist doctrine sometimes tends to do.

Even after conversion and the new birth, humans remain free, and sin remains real and powerful. For Wesley, the truth is that "sin remains but no longer reigns in the Christian." This calls Christians to resist sin with all our might, knowing that sin always has the potential of separating us from God.

With the basic distinctions hopefully clearly stated, let's look at some issues that all Christians need to consider thoughtfully and honestly, issues on which Calvinists and Methodists/Wesleyans have distinctively different perspectives.

The first is God's character.

We suggested earlier that a critical issue is which perspective, Calvinism or Arminianism, better represents the biblical picture of God's character and gives a more adequate account of the biblical God whose nature is holy love. The Calvinist understanding of divine sovereignty, which denies human free will and asserts that God's grace is restricted to a "chosen few," thus limiting the atonement of Christ to those chosen ones, necessarily raises turbulent questions as we read scripture and consider God's character.

How wide are God's saving intentions? Is not the whole world embraced by the loving heart of God described by John: "For God so loved the world that he gave his only Son" (John 3:16 NIV)? How can even the slightest restriction of to whom God's salvation mission is initiated be considered in the truth of that gospel word? In 1 John 2:2, we read that Jesus "is the atoning sacrifice for our sins, and not for ours only but also for the sins of the whole world." That doesn't sound like limited atonement. "God is love," says John, and "this is how God showed his love among us: He sent his only Son into the world . . . as an atoning sacrifice for our sins" (1 John 4:8-10 NIV).

All as the designation of those whom God loves and for whom he set in motion his saving mission in Jesus Christ is prominent throughout scripture. The first eleven chapters of the Epistle to the Romans describe the universal scope of human sin and disobedience. But the scope of God's merciful intention matches the scope of our fallenness: "For God has bound all men over to disobedience so that he may have mercy on them all" (Romans 11:32 NIV). Paul makes it clear that God's mercy is without exception.

A favorite "predestination passage" for the Calvinists is in the Epistle to the Romans: "For those whom he foreknew he also predestined to be conformed to the image of his Son. . . . And those whom he predestined he also called; and those whom he called he also justified; and those whom he justified he also glorified" (Romans 8:29-30). Of course, Wesleyans also affirm predestination and the crucial truth taught in this text, correctly interpreted. The issue is whether predestination is conditional or unconditional.

We discussed Wesley's argument against predestination in chapter 3. The reason for giving attention to this verse here is that it is in Romans, Paul's most reasoned theological statement. In the first three chapters of his letter, Paul establishes that all human beings without exception have been consigned to disobedience, and yet, as quoted above, Paul insists God intends to have mercy on all human beings without exception. Walls and Dongell convincingly contend that "even if we allow that Paul may here be referring to Jews and Gentiles as people groups, we must not imagine that God's desire to show mercy fails to apply to every individual within each group. After all, Paul establishes that all humans are under sin by arguing that both Gentiles (Rom. 1:18-32) and Jews (Rom. 2:1–3:20) as people groups are under sin. If we accept Paul's strategy of indicting every individual through indictment of the group, then consistency requires that we allow the same extension to hold with regard to God mercy, as Romans 11:32 seems to say" (*Why I Am Not a Calvinist*; p. 51).

Methodists/Wesleyans believe that the Calvinist account of the scope of the atonement limits the love of God and violates the witness of scripture. In fairness to the Calvinists, however, it must be noted that they believe the atonement is universal in value, sufficient to save everyone. The lynchpin, though, is that it is limited in scope, intended to save only the elect, and it does save them. We Methodists/Wesleyans believe that the atonement is not only universal in value; it is universal in intent, meant to save everyone, because this is who God is, full of mercy and always abounding in steadfast love.

Roger E. Olson expresses it in an interesting way. "Arminianism is all about protecting the reputation of God by protecting his character as revealed in Jesus Christ and Scripture. Arminians are not concerned about some humanly derived fascination with fairness; God does not have to be fair. Fairness is not necessary to goodness. But love and justice are necessary to goodness, and both exclude willing determination of sin, evil or eternal suffering" (*Arminian Theology*, p. 100).

So the character of God, not power or sovereignty, is the crucial issue. The universal extent of God's saving intention abounds in Scripture. "God our Savior, who wants all men to be saved and to come to a knowledge of the truth" (1 Timothy 2:3-4 NIV); "Christ Jesus, who gave himself as a ransom for all" (1 Timothy 2:5-6 NIV); "For the grace of God that brings salvation has appeared to all" (Titus 2:11 NIV). Since the use of *all* in these passages seems unqualified as relating to those God desires to save, it is difficult to even imagine God limiting his love.

Another distinctively different perspective between Calvinists and Methodists/Wesleyans is assurance. Assurance is one of the hallmarks of Protestant evangelical Christianity, the experience of knowing with certainty that we are redeemed from our sinful past.

Wesley labeled assurance "the privilege of all believers." We discussed this in chapter 5, but we need to consider it here in the particular context of Calvinism. Calvinists often claim that Arminians have no real basis for assurance in respect to their salvation. Those who make this claim have obviously not read John Wesley, who had a carefully worked out theology of assurance. Early in his ministry, Wesley believed that assurance was an essential aspect of our salvation; one was not "saved" who did not know he was "saved." Wesley modified this belief, concluding that though assurance is not necessary for salvation, it is "the privilege of all believers," and those who do not have the witness of the Spirit (assurance) as Christians are the exception rather than the rule. The norm was assurance. "Every Christian believer has a perceptible testimony of God's Spirit that he is a child of God" (a letter to John Smith, quoted by Kenneth J. Collins, *John Wesley: A Theological Journey*, Abingdon Press, 2003, p. 132).

Though the Calvinists claim that the doctrine of unconditional election provides a depth of certainty that Arminians lack, the question is how can that be? How is that witnessed to? R.C. Sproul, one of today's most popular apologists for Calvinism, confessed his struggle with this. In a moment of great self-awareness, he says, a dark question formed in his mind, and he was flooded with terror over the thought that perhaps he might not be one of God's redeemed. As he describes it, he began to think back over his own life, including the good and the bad; and the more he reflected, he says, the worse he felt. The thought that perhaps he was "not saved after all" was devastating. Then, he says,

> I went to my room and began to read the Bible. On my knees I said, "Well, here I am. I can't point to my obedience. There's nothing I can offer. . . ." I knew that some people only flee to the Cross to escape hell. . . . I could not be sure about my own heart and motivation. Then I remembered John 6:68, "Simon Peter answered him, 'Lord, to whom shall we go? You have the words of eternal life.'" Peter was also uncomfortable, but he realized that being uncomfortable with Jesus was better than any other option. ("Assurance of Salvation," Tabletalk, Ligonier Ministries, Inc., November, 1989; p. 20)

One can appreciate that kind of confession. Few Christians escape times of doubt concerning their salvation. When times of adversity come, when one experiences a moral failure, when self-examination reveals a cold heart and a weak and failing obedience, many sorts of struggles may send the believer into a dark period of questioning. Every pastor experiences this with those for whom he or she must offer pastoral care. Personal sensitivity is required, theological reflection cannot be avoided, and spiritual discernment is called for.

It is not enough to remind ourselves that it's a good sign to be worried, and only true Christians really care about salvation. It's not enough to share with Peter "being uncomfortable with Jesus." We can be assured of our relationship with Christ; this is our privilege as believers. "For you did not receive a spirit that makes you a slave again to fear, but you received the Spirit of sonship. And by him we cry, 'Abba, Father.' The Spirit himself testifies with our spirit that we are God's children" (Romans 8:15-16 NIV).

How can any Calvinist who believes in unconditional election and limited atonement know the peace and joy of the assurance which is the privilege of all believers? An answer may include something like this: If you are walking in cheerful obedience, if you are living before him with a clear conscience, if you are confident that despite your doubts you may always turn to Jesus who offers the divine promise of salvation. The answer demonstrates the problem. Everything in the answer has an unavoidable degree of subjectivity, and this is precisely the point at which believers struggle. They are questioning their salvation because they are not joyfully obedient; they do not have a clear conscience, and they are not confident in the divine promise of salvation.

The Calvinist cannot claim, nor can a Calvinist pastor offer to a struggling person, that he or she is loved by God with an electing love. If election is determined by God in eternity past and as J. I. Packer writes, "decreed by his counsel secret to us," how can such a belief ever make possible a doctrine of assurance? Calvinism deprives those struggling with their faith the confidence that God loves all of us with all and every kind of love we need to save us, to enable us to grow in our relationship to him, to mature in our obedience and discipleship, and to give us the joyful assurance that salvation is ours and nothing can separate us from the love of Christ Jesus, our Lord.

Walls and Dongell speak a sobering word:

> Calvinism lacks the clear warrant to speak the most liberating word of encouragement available for persons struggling with their faith and doubtful of God's attitude toward them . . . the unqualified assurance that God loves them and is for them! His love is such that he would never sovereignly choose to pass over any of his fallen children and leave them without hope of escaping the eternal misery of their sins. None need fear that the grace they have received only appears to be the real thing. If any are lost it is not because the grace God has provided is not adequate to save them. It is because they persistently and continually reject the love of the One whose mercy endures forever, a mercy they could indeed choose and receive. (*Why I Am Not a Calvinist;* p. 203)

We turn now to a final issue, *evangelism.* How can a Calvinist convincingly contend that God can have genuine compassion for persons he has not elected to save? Calvinist leaders like J. I. Packer and John Piper basically distance themselves from the traditional Reformed notion of limited atonement at this point, insisting that Christ died for all in the sense that his death is sufficient for all. They would even preach and teach that all are invited—indeed, commanded—to repent and believe. Pressed to explain, they would fall back on the conviction that electing love is unconditional, that Christ died for the elect in a sense different from his death for the non-elect. It is a "tough" truth to accept, and again questions the character of God and the universal intention of his saving mission in Jesus Christ. Calvinism says that Christ died "effectually" for those he chose from eternity to be saved. As the elect, God moves them to accept the offer of salvation. But those who are not elect cannot and will not accept the offer, so Christ's death is not "effectual" for them.

Apologists for Calvinism say they preach God's love for all because the natural and material blessings of God are "for all." They often use Jesus to prove their point. He said that God's love for all is proven in the fact that the rain falls on the just and the unjust alike (see Matthew 5:45). Though we accept that, what does it matter if material and temporal goods are lavished upon someone, if that person is denied the love of God that makes an eternal difference? Can we, with any convincing degree of honesty, prove God's love unless as a part of that love, what matters most—salvation and eternal life—is a possibility? Deep down it is clear to most, and the warning of Jesus strikes at our hearts: "What good will it be for a man if he gains the whole world, yet forfeits his soul?" (Matthew 16:26 NIV).

Calvinists answer those who might question motivation for evangelism in a theological system of unconditional election and limited atonement by calling to mind that God not only elects certain people to salvation, he ordains the means to their salvation—in other words, our preaching, praying, witnessing. If God ordains the means, then if I am to be the means, he will make me attentive, even passionate, about sharing the gospel. If I am not ordained to be the means, I can still be confident that the work of evangelism will get done without me. That's well and good, on the surface. But such thinking, in the least, diminishes the universal nature of Jesus' Great Commission: "All authority in heaven and on earth has been given to me. Therefore go and make disciples of all nations, baptizing them in the name of the Father and of the Son and of the Holy Spirit, and teaching them to obey everything I have commanded you. And surely I am with you always, to the very end of the age" (Matthew 28:18-20 NIV).

In closing, let me be clear. I write not to discredit Calvinism or to question the integrity of any apologist of that perspective. I write to make the case to those from a Calvinist perspective, as well as to Methodist/Wesleyan Christians who might be intimidated by the case made by Calvinists, that we out of the Arminian tradition are a dynamic part of Protestant evangelicalism. I want Calvinists to know that much of what they have been told about Arminians is false. We do believe in the sovereignty of God. We do believe in justification by grace through faith, and we do not attribute any spiritual goodness to human endeavor; salvation comes only by grace. I write also as an apologist for the Methodist/Wesleyan way, for our believing that the character of our almighty sovereign God, according to scripture, is not primarily a God of power, but of holy love. Our understanding and emphasis on grace and the universal offer of salvation, the gospel of assurance, and the call and possibility of holy living, personal and social, is a compelling theological perspective, and it offers the greatest potential for evangelism, mission, disciple-making, and fulfilling the Great Commission.

QUESTIONS FOR PERSONAL REFLECTION

1. Record the first five or six words that come to mind as you think about the nature and character of God.

2. Using the words you recorded to characterize God, rank the words in the order (1, 2, 3...) of which you think are most characteristic of God's nature.

3. Spend a few minutes seeking to recall Scripture passages, stories in Scripture, and parables or words of Jesus that relate to each of the word descriptions you listed.

4. The Wesleyan understanding of salvation involves the freedom of individuals to respond to the grace freely offered by God in Jesus Christ. Recall the first time you can remember responding to the grace of God, and briefly describe that experience.

5. The author writes, "We believe that saints do persevere, but they do so by the grace of God, and they do so by being vigilant in responding to God's grace, continually allowing the Holy Spirit to sensitize our consciences, and remaining absolutely dependent upon God's grace." What helps you to remain sensitive to the Holy Spirit and dependent upon God's grace? Reflect on the past week, month, or year; what are some specific ways you have responded to God's grace?

6. Reflecting on your response to the above questions, what does the witness of Scripture concerning the character of God and your Christian experience say about unconditional election, limited atonement, and irresistible grace? Make some notes.

7. Wesley said that "sin remains but no longer reigns in the Christian" (p. 146). He believed that this calls us to resist sin with all our might, knowing that sin always has the potential to separate us from God. Describe a recent time when sin separated you from God. How might you have resisted sin in this instance? What practices help you to resist sin "with all your might"?

8. Think back on the past few months; have you had any conversation in which the difference between Calvinism and the Wesleyan way was discussed? If so, what were the issues, and how did the discussion go? Spend a few minutes reflecting on how your study of this chapter will shape future similar conversations.

QUESTIONS FOR GROUP SHARING

1. Invite two or three people to share conversations they have had in which the difference between Calvinism and the Methodist/ Wesleyan way was discussed. What were the strongest disagreements? How might this week's study have helped them in those conversations?

2. What are some beliefs that both Calvinists and Arminians/ Wesleyans affirm?

3. Discuss how and why the concept of freedom is the primary distinction between Calvinist and Arminian theology. According to Calvinist theology, how might human freedom be seen as a threat to God's sovereignty? How does Arminian theology reconcile the concepts of human freedom and God's sovereignty?

4. Invite persons to respond to the author's statement that although God's sovereignty and power are important issues, the fundamental issue is God's holy love. Discuss why the concept of God's holy love is critical to our understanding of who God is, what God has done through Jesus Christ, and how God calls us to respond.

5. Read the paragraphs on pp. 144–146, beginning with "Calvinism contends that God has chosen to rescue certain specific fallen sinners. . . ." Contrast the Calvinist principles of unconditional election, limited atonement, and irresistible grace with John Wesley's ideas about God's prevenient and universal grace and our freedom to respond.

6. Read John 3:16-18; 1 John 2:2, 4:8-10; 1 Timothy 2:3-6; Titus 2:11; and Romans 5:6-8; 11:32. According to these verses, how wide are God's saving intentions? Are there any exceptions to God's mercy?

7. How does the idea of the perseverance of the saints ("eternal security") differ from John Wesley's ideas about assurance of salvation, which he said was "the privilege of all believers"?

8. In what ways might the principles of unconditional election and limited atonement diminish the universal nature of Jesus' Great Commission (see Matthew 28:18-20)? In contrast, how should the ideas of God's universal love and grace and human beings' free will motivate us for evangelism and missions?

9. Spend the balance of your time together talking about any issues that have been raised during the course of this study, and especially any issues that call for more discussion or action. Also, consider where your group may go from here. Have you considered seeing this group as an ongoing means of grace in your life together—"going on to salvation"?